JENNI CALDER was ... England, and has lived ... years of part-time teaching and freelance writing, including three years in Kenya, she worked at the National Museums of Scotland from 1978 to 2001 successively as education officer, Head of Publications, script editor for the Museum of Scotland, and latterly as Head of Museum of Scotland International. In the latter capacity her main interest was in emigration and the Scottish diaspora. She has written and lectured widely on Scottish, English and American literary and historical subjects, and writes fiction and poetry as Jenni Daiches. She has two daughters, a son and a dog.

Frontier Scots
The Scots who won the West

JENNI CALDER

A man didn't make history, staying close to home.
A.B. GUTHRIE JR, *The Way West*

It is the settlers, after all, at whom we have a right to marvel.
R.L. STEVENSON, *Across the Plains*

Luath Press Limited
EDINBURGH
www.luath.co.uk

First published 2010

ISBN: 978-1-906307-99-8

The paper used in this book is recyclable. It is made from
low chlorine pulps produced in a low energy, low emissions manner
from renewable forests.

Printed and bound by
Bell & Bain Ltd., Glasgow

Maps by Jim Lewis

Typeset in 10 point Sabon
by 3btype.com

Cover: Photograph of the Matador Outfit Eating at the Chuck Wagon at the
Time. Murdo Mackenzie, centre with black hat and beard, took over the
management of the ranch. At the extreme right is Henry H. 'Paint'
Campbell who established the ranch in 1879 with a half-dugout for
headquarters. Matador Ranch, Texas. 1905–10, gelatin dry plate negative.
© Erwin E. Smith Foundation, Erwin E. Smith Collection of the Library
of Congress on Deposit at the Amon Carter Museum, Fort Worth,
Texas, LC.S61.003

Contents

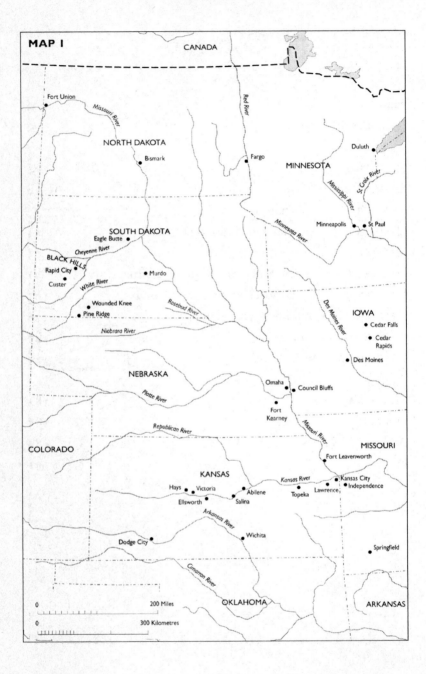

MAP I

MAP 2

COLORADO

KANSAS

MISSOURI

Fort Leavenworth

Kansas River

Kansas City

Independence

Hays

Abilene

Topeka

Lawrence

Ellsworth

Salina

Arkansas River

Wichita

Dodge City

Medicine Lodge

Springfield

Cimarron River

Adobe Walls

Canadian River

Tulsa

ARKANSAS

Guthrie

Oklahoma City

McLean

OKLAHOMA

NEW
MEXICO

Fort
Sumner

Red River

Peace
River

Duncan

Matador

Lubbock

Guthrie

Dallas

Sabine River

Brazos River

Trinity River

Nacogdoces

LOUISIANA

TEXAS

Colorado River

Pecos River

Austin

Lockhart

Houston

San Antonio

Gonzales

Galveston

Nueces River

Corpus Christi

Gulf of Mexico

MEXICO

Rio Grande

Brownsville

0 — 200 Miles

0 — 300 Kilometres

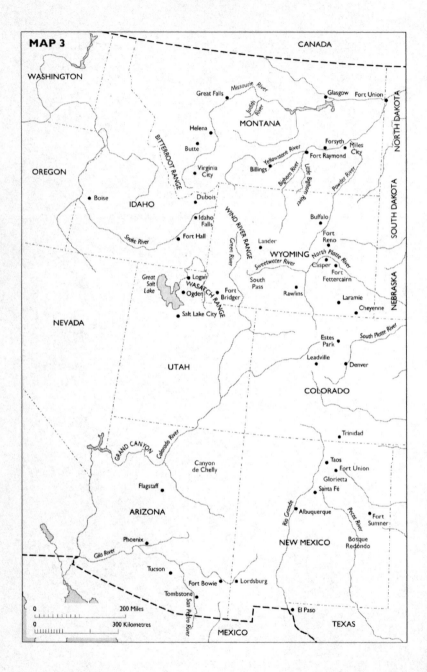

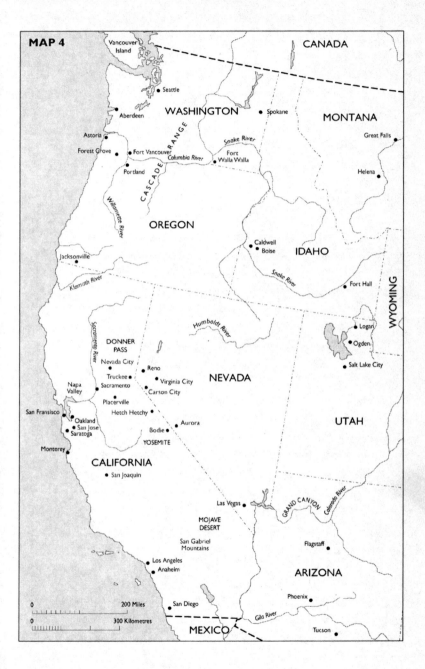

MAP 4

Introduction

IN 1842, JOHN REGAN, from Ayrshire, took passage from Liverpool to New Orleans and made his way up the Mississippi River to Burlington, Iowa. He settled on the Spoon River in Illinois, purchasing 40 acres of land for £10 sterling, on which he grew corn and raised pigs. It was hard work. He built an 18-by-14-foot house, ploughed, sowed, harvested and threshed his corn, and took it to market. Cutting firewood was a major task – the winters were long and cold. His wife made bread, butter, soap and candles, spun flax and wool, and made the family's clothes. She also got a job as a teacher to bring in some cash. In his book *The Western Wilds of America* (1859) Regan wrote:

> In that western country a man who feels himself unable or disin-
> clined to strike in boldly with his own hands, and help himself,
> will find himself continually behind... the immigrant must be a
> man of action – be first and last in everything. If he cannot do a
> thing well, let him do it nevertheless, and wait on no one for aid,
> if aid be scarce.

The Regans were among the thousands who left Scotland in the first half of the 19th century and made their way to what was then the Far West. Most of them travelled as families and individuals rather than as groups. Unlike Canada, the US saw few settlements of whole communities from Scotland and as Scottish Americans followed the frontier, they became increasingly dispersed. Their neighbours might come from anywhere in Europe, or they might have no neighbours at all. The settler, Regan said, had 'to learn life anew', adapt to an alien landscape and an existence among strangers. At first Regan was homesick, but gradually that faded: 'Every year the settler passes in the new country, he is striking his roots more widely and firmly into the soil, and his attachments to the far-off land wither and decay, till at last he has nothing of regrets to trouble him.'

Yet often immigrants did not stay long enough in one place to grow roots. They might settle initially in one of the eastern states, then cross the Appalachians to Kentucky or Tennessee, then move on again as new territories were opened up. They were undeterred by vast distances and difficult journeys. In 1793, Scottish-born James Stuart was an Indian trader on the frontiers of the newly formed United States of America. His son Robert married Nancy Currence Hall, and they had two sons, James and Granville. Granville was born in Clarksburg, Virginia, in August 1834. Three years later the family headed west. From Wheeling, not far from Clarksburg, they took a steamboat down the Ohio River to the Mississippi, where another steamboat took them north to Rock Island, upriver from Burlington. The last stage of their journey, by wagon, took them a short distance east to Princeton, near the Illinois River. From Wheeling to Princeton took them a month.

Robert Stuart, second-generation Scottish American, stayed only a year in Illinois before moving his family west again, across the Mississippi to Iowa. There, he took up land claim number 16 on a creek called the Wapsanohock – 'crooked creek' in the Musquawkee language. There, Robert built a one-room log cabin, and the boys played with the local Indian children. The school they went to was a log cabin with an earth floor.

Five years later the family moved again, to a farm on the Red Cedar River, near what is now Cedar Falls but was then the edge of wilderness. Granville and James learned to hunt, fish and canoe. In 1849 news of gold strikes in California caused huge excitement. Like thousands of others, Robert Stuart, with three companions, set off on the overland trek across the Great Plains and the Rocky Mountains for the gold fields. They reached the Sacramento valley in the autumn of that year. After two years of no great success Robert returned home, this time travelling by ship to Nicaragua, crossing to the Gulf of Mexico, another ship to New Orleans and then up the Mississippi. But the following year he headed west again, taking his two sons. They set off with two light-spring wagons, each pulled by four horses, loaded with supplies and spare clothing, bedding and weapons. They slept in the wagons. As Granville would write years later, 'after many annoyances and much profanity' they arrived at Council Bluffs on the 'wide swift flowing muddy' Missouri River. For $10 per wagon and team, an exorbitant price, they were ferried across the river, and continued the long, arduous and often dangerous journey to California.

The progress of the Stuart family, from Virginia where many Scots settled, moving west as new territories opened up, and the career of Granville Stuart in particular, encapsulate many of the experiences of Scottish Americans who followed the frontier. Granville will make many appearances in the chapters that follow. He had a typical pioneer upbringing. He was 18 when he went to California, where he and his brother James staked their claims and prospected for gold. Later, Granville would be a trader, a cattleman, a vigilante, a land agent and a politician. At the age of 70 he became librarian of the public library at Butte, Montana, and at 84 he was commissioned to write a history of the state. His life spanned a period of extraordinary change, which saw the American West settled and the frontier tamed: in 1890 it was declared officially closed by the US Census Board. By that time Native Americans were confined to reservations, towns and their institutions were burgeoning, fortunes had been won and lost, communications transformed. Towards the end of his life Granville wrote:

> I have seen the tide of emigration sweep from the Mississippi river to the Pacific coast, and from the Rio Grande to Alaska. I can remember when there was not a single railroad west of the Mississippi, when there was not a telephone or telegraph line in existence, and a tallow dip was our best means of illumination.

In his memoir, *Forty Years on the Frontier* (1925), he portrays himself as a rugged and acute frontiersman who made a significant contribution to conquering the wilderness. Whatever his own agenda, it remains a valuable source.

Charles Mackay visited the US in the 1850s, and responded excitedly. 'It is on American soil that the highest destinies of civilisation will be wrought out to their conclusions,' he wrote, 'and the record of what is there doing, however often the story may be told, will be always interesting and novel. Progress crawls in Europe, but gallops in America.'

For those who at that time were beginning to infiltrate the trans-Missouri west, 'gallops' was an appropriate word, as horses played so significant a role in the events of the last phase of the frontier. Thirty years later Lord Bryce commented: 'The West is the most American part of America... the part where those features which distinguish America from Europe come out in the strongest relief.' The Scottish input to the frontier character and its legacy was considerable.

Scots played a significant part in every stage of American history. In the colonial period Scottish merchants and ministers, lawyers and doctors, and perhaps above all teachers, were prominent and influential. Scottish ideas crossed the Atlantic in books and in people's heads, and were absorbed by those who shaped the Declaration of Independence and the American Constitution. Scottish people were seen as reliable and hard-working settlers, opening up the wilderness and securing it. That legacy remained with the next generations, as the Stuart family exemplify.

In the 19th century, Scots were among the millions of Europeans who poured into the United States and provided labour for the mines and factories, and homesteaders for the newly-opened territories. They explored the Far West and were key players in the fur trade that brought the first Europeans to the Rockies and the Pacific Northwest. Appropriately, in Steven Spielberg's 2006 television series *Into the West* there are identifiable Scots among the mountain men portrayed in the first episode. One of them sells a captive Cheyenne woman to the hero Jake Wheeler: Thunder Heart

Woman becomes Jake's wife. And viewers familiar with the novels and film scripts of A.B. Guthrie Jr. (the name is Angus in origin) were no doubt amused to note that one of Spielberg's overlanders is called – A.B. Guthrie jr. Another Guthrie, Woody, ensured that the folk record of cowboy life survived, in songs such as 'The Chisholm Trail', 'Billy the Kid' and 'Whoopee Ti Yi Yo', songs that themselves often reflected the influence of a Scottish tradition.

Scots fought on both sides in the Civil War, as they had done in the Revolutionary War. They fought Native Americans, and championed them. They were law makers and law breakers. As new communities were planted west of the Missouri, they established businesses and institutions. They helped to develop the commercial potential of ranching, mining and railroads, providing money, managerial and banking skills, and imagination, as well as labour. They are prominent in the history of the American West, and also in its myths and in the fiction and films it has generated.

In the 1890s, around a hundred years after James Stuart settled in Virginia, a group of Scottish families from Dundee made their way to Montana, where in the Big Belt Hills, not far from Helena, they settled and farmed. As far as Helena they were able to travel by train, but the last stage of their journey was by wagon on a rough country track. Although by this time the American frontier was deemed to be closed and Model T Fords would soon be bumping along that track, their life in the Montana hills was not so different from that of the Stuarts in Illinois and Iowa. The wilderness was still there. On the mountain pastures they raised sheep and fended off the wolves and coyotes. They made the most of the summer months and battled through savage winters. Their story is told by Ivan Doig, the grandson of one of them, in his memoir, *This House of Sky* (1987). It is a story indelibly stamped with a Scottish inheritance. Ivan's father, Charles Doig, who was born in Montana and worked in the mountains all his life, never lost the Scottish timbre of his voice. Ivan's writing is imbued with the resonance of his Scottish origins and the experience of his pioneer forebears.

Scots made good pioneers. They were ubiquitously characterised as tough, courageous and hardworking. Many were Presbyterians, which predisposed them to a pragmatic endurance and a faith in survival, even when long separated from the accustomed manifestations of religion. Many were Highlanders, formed by a terrain as demanding if not on the same scale as the American West. Some had been schooled in the equally unforgiving environment of the Industrial Revolution. The Scottish soldier was a presence in all America's wars, before and after the Revolution. Many pioneer communities could produce a fiddler to perform when celebrations were in order, and that fiddler, if not a Scot himself, would likely owe his style and his music to a Celtic tradition.

Scots also relished the scope for freedom of thought and action which they found on the frontier. There is no doubt that some abused the opportunities that came their way, helped themselves to land, exploited those less fortunate than themselves, and assisted in the destruction of the native population. But they were also conspicuous among the heroes and heroines of the frontier (although the records inevitably have much less to say about the latter), sung and unsung. They were adventurous and astute explorers and innovators as well as tenacious travellers and homesteaders.

In his book *America Revisited* (1905), David Macrae commented specifically on Scots in the West. 'America is another Scotland on a huge scale,' he said. And he added, 'America would have been a poor show if it had not been for the Scottish.' There is scarcely an episode in the dramatic and resonant story of the American West in which Scots do not appear. That resonance reaches back across the Atlantic, for North America is part of Scotland's history. The bagpipes that were heard on the walls of the Alamo, the Gaelic spoken by Montana cowboys, the volume of Robert Burns's poetry carried by John Muir on his long walks, these belong with the continuing narrative of Scotland's past.

CHAPTER I

Trailblazers

Give me a home in the far, far west;
That's the place I love the best.

'The Far, Far West', traditional,
as remembered by J. E. McCauley, Texas

ON 24 APRIL 1813 a small party of men reached Fort Osage on the Missouri River. They had crossed the Rocky Mountains from the Pacific coast. They were led by a man called Robert Stuart, who had grown up in the parish of Callander on the edge of the Scottish Highlands. While thousands were heading west from the eastern states, they had travelled 2,000 miles in the opposite direction from a part of the American continent almost unknown to white people.

Stuart and six men had left the fur trading post of Astoria, near the mouth of the Columbia River, in June of the previous year, entrusted with carrying dispatches to New York. The dispatches reported on the progress of the trading enterprise initiated by John Jacob Astor who had founded the American Fur Company in 1808 and had plans to expand. He decided to challenge the dominance of the British North West Company, which had outposts in the Columbia River area, and for this purpose he recruited men, several poached from the rival company, to set up Astoria. The plan was for Astoria (in present-day Oregon) to become a focus of trading activities, gathering in furs from a vast hinterland and loading them on ships. Some would make the long and difficult voyage round Cape Horn to the east coast; others, it was hoped, would sail west and supply the oriental demand for furs.

All the men with Robert Stuart were experienced frontiersmen; two of them were also Scots. Robert McClellan, though Pennsylvania born, was a Highlander by descent. As a young man he had led pack trains across the Alleghenies, the mountains that marked the first frontier of the American colonies. For a while he was an army scout. William Clark – who with Meriwether Lewis led the first US expedition to cross the Rockies east to west and was himself of Scottish extraction – described him as 'brave, honest and sincere, an intrepid warrior'. He also had a volatile temper. Ramsay Crooks had been born in Greenock on the River Clyde, the son of a shoemaker. In 1803, at the age of 16, he accompanied his widowed mother to Montreal. Three years later he was engaged in the fur trade with McClellan, along the upper reaches of the Missouri. The two men established a trading post at Calhoun, Nebraska. When they joined Astor's venture in 1811 they were veterans of the wilderness – mountain men, as the few white men who had penetrated the Rockies were called.

When Washington Irving was asked by J.J. Astor to write an account of Astoria's short but action-packed life he responded with enthusiasm. He celebrated an episode of hardship and adventure, which opened the way to settlement and the expansion of the young United States of America. The fur hunters were the vanguard, who blazed trails that would eventually 'carry the American population across the Rocky Mountains and spread it along the shores of the Pacific':

> Without pausing on the borders, they have penetrated at once, in defiance of difficulties and dangers, to the heart of savage countries; laying open the hidden secrets of the wilderness; leading the way to remote regions of beauty and fertility that might have remained unexplored for ages, and beckoning after them the slow and pausing steps of agriculture and civilisation.

Irving was himself the son of a Scot, William Irving from Shapinsay in Orkney, who had emigrated to New York in 1763. In his account, he highlighted the fact that Scots were the engine of the fur trade conducted by the North West Company and the Hudson's Bay Company, as partners, as traders, as factors of remote trading posts deep in the wilderness, and as explorers. When Astor launched his subsidiary Pacific Fur Company in 1810, it was almost inevitable that his expedition to the Pacific would be manned by Scots. Laurence Oliphant, a Scot who visited the US in the early 1850s, stressed the stamina and toughness of Scots involved in the fur trade, and also their 'shrewdness and sagacity' in harnessing the skills of the *voyageurs* who were vital to North West Company success.

Robert Stuart was a tall, dark-haired, prepossessing man, the son of a crofter and schoolmaster, who had first tried to make his way as a teacher. His uncle, David Stuart, was one of many Highlanders recruited by the North West Company, and when Robert's father died in 1807 David suggested that Robert should join him at the company's headquarters in Montreal. Robert was offered a post as clerk, which involved checking beaver pelts before their export to Europe. Montreal was the hub of the fur trade, where the Nor'Wester partners gathered for sumptuous and riotous dinners and drinking sessions, but Robert's role was modest and dull. When John Jacob Astor came to Montreal looking for recruits for his proposed Pacific coast venture both Robert and his uncle were keen to sign up. There were plenty of their compatriots of like mind. Their fellow adventurers included Alexander Mckay and his son Tom; Donald Mackenzie, a cousin of Alexander Mackenzie, the first explorer to cross the continent; Duncan McDougall, and Alexander Ross.

Irving described the Scots in general as 'characterised by the perseverance, thrift, and fidelity of their country, and fitted by their native hardihood to encounter the rigorous climate of the north, and to endure the trials and privations of their lot'. Alexander Mckay had accompanied Mackenzie on both his expeditions. Donald Mackenzie had 10 years' experience with the North West Company, and as well as having a good knowledge of 'Indian trade and Indian warfare' was 'seasoned to toils and hardships' with 'a spirit not to be intimidated'. He was also an excellent shot. Later, Ramsay Crooks and Robert McClellan were taken on.

Astor proposed two expeditions, one overland and one by sea, sailing south and rounding Cape Horn into the Pacific. It would be hard to say which journey was the more hazardous. In September, 1810, David and Robert Stuart, the Mckays, McDougall and Ross boarded the *Tonquin* in New York, along with a cargo of tools and materials to build a trading post, weapons and ammunition, and goods – cloth, axes, knives, fishing tackle, kettles, frying pans – to trade with the natives. From the start there were problems. Captain Jonathan Thorn did not care for the Scots (as well as members of the expedition there were Scots among the crew) or for the French Canadian *voyageurs* who were also on board. He did not like the fact that the Scots spoke Gaelic and the *voyageurs* spoke French, neither of which he could understand. He was stubborn and autocratic, a man of 'a jealous and peevish temper,' according to Alexander Ross, and seemed particularly to dislike Robert Stuart. The *Tonquin*'s months at sea were filled with friction, and at times confrontation.

After a difficult voyage, the following spring the *Tonquin* eventually arrived at the mouth of the Columbia River and faced the notoriously treacherous sandbanks that guarded it. Thorn's determination to enter the river, in spite of high winds and a heavy sea, resulted in the loss of eight lives and nearly of the ship. But landfall was eventually made on the southern bank of the estuary, and the business of clearing the thickly wooded site was begun. Alexander Ross, whose account of the expedition, *Adventures of the First Settlers on the Oregon or Columbia River*, was published in 1849, felt that it would have been hard to find a more problematic site for 'the emporium of the west':

> [it was] studded with gigantic trees of almost incredible size, many of them measuring 50 feet in girth, and so close together, and intermingled with huge rocks, as to make it a work of no ordinary labour to level and clear the ground.

While the 'no ordinary labour' of creating Astoria was going on, supervised by Duncan McDougall, Captain Thorn continued up the coast, hoping to trade with the natives. He and all but one of those on board, including Alexander Mckay, were never seen again. Eventually it was learnt that they were killed by Indians on Vancouver Island.

It took two months to clear an acre and prepare a site for a trading post. Felling trees and constructing buildings were just the beginning. Contacts had to be made with those who would supply the beaver pelts on which success depended. For this purpose, an expedition set off up the majestic Columbia River, following it to the east, then bending sharply to the north, until they reached the confluence with the Okanogan, which crosses into what is now Canada. With half the party David Stuart continued up the Okanogan, where he established another trading post. Washington Irving's comment strikes a heroic note:

> In the heart of savage and unknown country, 700 miles from the main body of his fellow-adventurers, Stuart had dismissed half his little number, and was prepared with the residue to brave all the perils of the wilderness, and rigours of a long and dreary winter.

Alexander Ross, who was for a spell left at the confluence of the rivers with only a small dog called Weasel for companionship, tells us rather more about the experience of survival in 'this unhallowed wilderness', as he called it, 'without friend or white man within hundreds of miles of me, and surrounded by savages who had never seen a white man before'.

> Every day seemed a week, every night a month. I pined, I lan-guished, my head turned grey, and in a brief space 10 years were added to my age. Yet man is born to endure, and my only conso-lation was in my Bible.

Although reliance on the bible was perhaps not typical of the mountain men, it provides an insight into a strain of the Scottish character which was a source of fortitude. Many emigrant Scots brought their religious conviction with them, whether Presbyterian, Catholic or Episcopalian, and for thousands of settlers it was a mainstay. But Ross's comments on his fellow fur-traders were caustic. In his view they were 'dissolute spendthrifts who spin out, in feasting and debauchery, a miserable existence, neither fearing God nor regarding man, till the knife of the savage, or some other violent death, despatches them unpitied'. It is perhaps not surprising to find Ross pleading for resources to evangelise the natives, whom he regarded as more promising material than the white men who first encroached on their territory. Unlike the latter, the Indians in his view exhibited 'a strong desire and capacity for receiving moral and religious instruction'.

While David Stuart was setting up a trading post on the Okanogan, in the northern part of central Washington, his nephew Robert was exploring the Willamette Valley nearer the coast, which would later attract large numbers of settlers. Stuart reported that the area was 'delightful beyond expression', full of potential for farmers. But at Astoria, things were not going well. Many of the men working on clearing the site had never handled an axe; some had never handled a gun. Both were essential tools. The autumn of 1811 brought a shortage of food, and the prospects for winter were not encouraging. However, the trading post's first New Year was celebrated with some gusto. Duncan McDougall recorded the day in his journal:

> At sunrise, the drums beat to arms and the colours were hoisted. Three rounds of small arms and three discharges from the great guns were fired, after which all hands were treated to grog, bread, cheese and butter...

When the sun went down another salvo was fired and there was dancing until three in the morning. Seventeen days later the first group of Astor's overland expedition, including Donald Mackenzie and Robert McClellan, finally reached the end of an epic journey. Four weeks later, the canoes of the rest of the party appeared. Weak and demoralised, they had battled through snowstorms, fended off Indian attacks, and negotiated the rapids and whirlpools of the most formidable rivers of the northwest, latterly living on little but beaver skins.

The overland party was led by William Hunt, a 27 year old American based in St Louis who had the task of recruiting in Montreal and Michilimackinac, between Lakes Huron and Michigan, and then in St Louis, the real starting point. It took weeks to equip the expedition. They needed horses and provisions, weapons and ammunition, and trade goods. They had to be prepared for hostile Indians, and also for rival fur traders. They were competing not only with the North West Company, but with the St Louis Fur Company who had their eye on the headwaters of the Missouri and were suspicious of the Astorians.

It was late in October before they set off up the Missouri. It was the following July before they struck west across the prairies: the five partners, Hunt, McClellan, Crooks, Mackenzie, and Joseph Miller, a Missouri trader; 45 French Canadian *engagés*, and 11 trapper-hunters. Most of the 82 horses were needed to carry baggage; everyone except the partners was on foot. Ahead, beyond a vast stretch of dry prairie, were range upon range of mountains, unpredictable rivers, uncertain food supplies, and possibly hostile Indians. In the course of the ordeal that followed they suffered near-starvation, desperate thirst and sickness. They were helped by some Indians, harassed by others. They relied on fragments of information to find their way, and frequently had to backtrack when a chosen route proved impossible. Eventually, with winter approaching, they reached the Snake River (in Idaho) but did not know whether to follow it up or downriver. As Washington Irving put it:

> They were in the heart of an unknown wilderness, untraversed as yet by a white man. They were at a loss what route to take, and how far they were from the ultimate place of their destination, nor could they meet, in these uninhabited wilds, with any human being to give them information.

Hunt split the party into three, led by McClellan, Crooks and

Mackenzie. One party went upriver, another down, while the third headed north. The snows came. There was no game, and they had to eat their horses. Mackenzie and McClellan at last reached the Columbia River, to arrive at Astoria on 18 January. It was nearly a month before the remainder of Hunt's expedition finally made it.

Yet the potential for trade was real. Beaver were plentiful, the local tribes, in spite of some hostility and suspicion, were sufficiently co-operative, and though sorely tested by the ordeals of getting there, there was no lack of courage and determination amongst the incomers. A serious challenge to success, however, came from the North West Company, the former employer of many of the men, whose ambitions and energy showed no sign of dwindling. Not long after the Astorians had begun to get themselves established, a canoe was seen making its way downriver towards the embryonic trading post. In it was David Thompson, one of the North West Company's partners, who had been visiting a Nor'Wester post recently set up near what became Spokane. Those involved were John MacTavish, a relative of Simon MacTavish, founder of the North West Company whose fur-trading career had begun in Albany, New York, burly red-haired Finan MacDonald from Lochaber, and Jacques Finlay, a Scottish Métis. Macdonald and Finlay had accompanied Thompson (who was Welsh) on his epic 1807 journey to the mouth of the Columbia River.

Astor had originally attempted to defuse possible rivalry with the Nor'Westers by inviting them to become involved with his enterprise. At first they had declined; now David Thompson was accepting the offer. But rivalry didn't just concern those competing for furs. Britain and the US both had their eye on the potentially lucrative northwest, and with boundaries undefined and the area largely unmapped the activities of those carving out routes through the wilderness and setting up trading posts had a political dimension. In 1803 Thomas Jefferson had successfully negotiated the Louisiana Purchase which vastly expanded US territory south and west. At this stage there was not a great deal of interest in the prairies, but the

Pacific northwest was another matter, offering potential for settlement as well as for trade, and a route to the west and the markets of the orient.

It would be over 40 years before the matter was settled and Britain gave up claim to Oregon and Washington Territories. But first there was a war, which in 1812 involved an attempt by the US to invade Canada (British North America as it was then designated) with the hope, if not the expectation, that Canadians would embrace American liberty. The war made little impact either on the Scots of the North West Company or those of Astor's American Fur Company. Their priorities were commercial rather than political, if indeed their main concern was not simply staying alive.

The war, inconsequential in outcome, certainly made no difference to Robert Stuart. On 29 June 1812, not knowing that five days before the first shots of a war between Britain and the United States had been fired, Robert Stuart, with his six men, set off with their dispatches for New York. They made their way up the Columbia River to the confluence with the Walla Walla and then struck north for Spokane. A Shoshone guide indicated that there was a route through the Rockies to the south of that taken by Hunt and his men through the Tetons. But the threat of attack from Crow Indians deterred Stuart and he decided to aim for Hunt's route. In spite of this diversion the Crows raided and stole their horses. Crooks was ill, and a quarrel with McClellan resulted in the latter storming off on his own. It proved a gruelling and useless detour, but finally, with help from more Shoshone, Stuart crossed the Continental Divide through South Pass. It would be the route that 30 or so years later thousands of emigrants would take in the opposite direction.

Stuart was through the mountains but his problems were not over. They had run out of food and hoped for buffalo, but were at first disappointed. They found McClellan, on the edge of starvation, 'worn to a perfect skeleton', and struggled on. Stuart had no illusions about the nature of the challenge:

> The phantoms which haunt a desert are want, misery and danger, the evils of dereliction rush upon the mind. Man is unwillingly acquainted with his own weakness, and meditation shows him only how little he can sustain, and how little he can perform.

It was perhaps this humility in the face of an unrelenting landscape that enabled him to carry on.

Finally, they reached the Sweetwater and followed it to the North Platte. It was November, and Stuart decided to over-winter beside the river, near present-day Casper, Wyoming. In five months they had travelled more than 2,000 miles. But they became aware of Arapaho Indians in the area, and decided to move on. They passed the confluence of the Laramie and North Platte Rivers, where 20 or so years later Robert Campbell and William Sublette would build a trading post, which became Fort Laramie. They halted a little further on near present-day Torrington, close to the border with Nebraska. They celebrated the New Year of 1813 with a feast of buffalo. They had run out of tobacco, so smoked the cut-up remnants of a tobacco pouch.

In March, Stuart and his band resumed their journey, following the Platte River east until they reached the Missouri on 18 April. Six days later they arrived at Fort Osage, the only US garrison west of the Mississippi. Ten months after leaving Astoria Stuart was in St Louis, where quite a stir was caused by the first news of William Hunt, who had left St Louis 18 months earlier, and developments at Astoria. There was also excitement at the route Stuart and his men had taken across the Divide. The *Missouri Gazette* reported:

> By information received from these gentlemen, it appears that a journey across the continent of N. America, might be performed with a wagon, there being no obstruction on the whole route that any person would dare to call a mountain in addition to its being much the most direct and short one to go from this place to the mouth of the Columbia River.

Stuart still had a long way to go. He left St Louis on horseback, and headed east through Missouri, Illinois, Indiana and Kentucky, and then continued by stagecoach. He arrived in New York on 23 June. From coast to coast had taken him a year.

Stuart's report to John Jacob Astor soon became irrelevant. The opportunistic Nor'Westers took matters into their own hands. John McTavish arrived at Astoria where Duncan McDougall and Donald Mackenzie made the decision to abandon the venture and sell up to the North West Company. A British frigate was expected any day to reinforce the message conveyed by McTavish that there was little to be gained by resisting the Nor'westers. McDougall returned to employment in his former company. Washington Irving commented regretfully on the debacle. Under the United States, he said, 'the country would have been explored and settled by industrious husbandmen; and the fertile valleys, bordering its rivers, and shut up among its mountains, would have been made to pour forth their agricultural treasure to contribute to the general wealth.' He envisaged 'a line of trading posts from the Mississippi and the Missouri across the Rocky Mountains, forming a high road from the great regions of the west to the shores of the Pacific'. But although a setback for the US, the territories of Oregon and Washington did of course become American, and some, at least, of what Irving envisaged came to pass.

By the time Irving's account was published there were already several forts established, many with Scottish connections. Astoria itself was renamed Fort George, then abandoned. In 1825, the Hudson's Bay Company, which by this time had taken over the North West Company, set up an impressive new post 100 miles upriver, above the mouth of the Willamette. Fort Vancouver would play a key role not only in the fur trade but in the early decades of settlement in Oregon. It was presided over by the redoubtable, larger-than-life Dr John McLoughlin, a Quebec-born Scot with a medical degree from Edinburgh University, who had married the widow of Astorian Alexander McKay, killed when the *Tonquin* was attacked at Nootka on Vancouver Island. McLoughlin performed a tricky balancing act, maintaining the supremacy of the Hudson's Bay Company in the face of increasing American fur trading encroachment, while frequently assisting the American pioneers who were crossing the Continental Divide in increasing numbers. His employers, however, were not keen to make American settlement in Oregon easier.

Fort Vancouver was a community in itself, with extensive buildings and warehouses, a church and a jail. Ocean-going ships came up the river with supplies and departed with their cargo of furs. McLoughlin cultivated orchards and grew vegetables with which he often fed destitute emigrants. The Astorians would have found it all difficult to imagine. Further north, near what would become the border with Canada, was Fort Colvile also on the Columbia, which curves northwards where it is met by the Snake River. Fort Colvile was established in 1826. Sent there as an apprentice clerk in 1839 was a young man called Angus MacDonald from Torridon, Wester Ross, a nephew of Archibald MacDonald who was already well established in the fur trade. Angus MacDonald was tall and black-haired, and appears as the quintessential mountain man. He wore buckskins, became a skilled horseman and marksman, and acquired a thorough knowledge of wilderness survival skills. He spoke, as well as his native Gaelic, English, French and several Indian languages, and was immersed in Indian culture and legend. His wife Catherine was a Nez Perce.

Fort Union, on the Missouri near the mouth of the Yellowstone, was founded in 1828 by Kenneth Mackenzie. Mackenzie had emigrated from Ross-shire 10 years earlier, at the age of 21. He worked for the Columbia Fur Company based in St Louis. When, in 1827, it merged with the American Fur Company he was put in control of the Upper Missouri and pioneered trade with the Blackfeet. The fur trade was highly dependent on good relations with native tribes, as they supplied the furs. Although there were independent white trappers, they were officially discouraged. The bulk of the furs was brought in by the Indians who traded them for a range of goods, including blankets and kettles, weapons and ammunition, and alcohol. The latter was illegal, but still found its way into Native American hands. Mackenzie himself ran into trouble when he established an illicit distillery at Fort Union. Later, he made a success of a legal liquor business, and did well from the land-speculation boom that came with the railroad.

The Scots seemed to have a talent for establishing good relations with native peoples. The success of the North West Company and the Hudson's Bay Company relied on this, and many Scots sealed their connections with individual tribes by marrying Indian women. Most of these unions were without benefit of clergy and many did not survive. But others did – Angus and Catherine MacDonald are a good example. Such partnerships were accepted in frontier situations, but were often problematic in 'civilised' social environments, and their children could have a difficult time. A recurrent theme in frontier literature concerns the 'half-breed', who feels he or she has no place in either Indian or white society. There were exceptions, particularly notable in Canada. James Douglas, son of a Scot and a black Caribbean woman who became governor of British Columbia, had an Indian wife, as did Moray-born Donald Smith, Lord Strathcona, politician, businessman and driving force behind the Canadian Pacific Railway.

Angus and Catherine MacDonald remained on the frontier, from 1846 ranching in Montana. They made sure their son Duncan was taught to read and write, and the family, including surviving descendants, stressed the importance of education. It was seen as a very Scottish concern, and often cited as a reason for the impact of Scots in North America. Duncan MacDonald would play an important mediating role in the Indian wars of the 1870s, in which his skill in articulating the cause of his mother's people was striking.

Archibald MacDonald, a 21-year-old from Glencoe, was recruited by Lord Selkirk, who believed that a solution for the economic ills of the Highlands was to facilitate settlement on the other side of the Atlantic. One of his schemes involved transplanting families from

Kildonan in Sutherland to the banks of the Red River in what would become Manitoba. In June 1813, shortly after Robert Stuart finally made it to New York with dispatches from Astoria, MacDonald led his group of 94 men, women and children on board two Hudson's Bay Company ships which were to take them across the Atlantic. It was the start of an extraordinary epic journey that lasted for more than a year. Many died on the way and there would be many more years of struggle before the community was securely established. Eventually the city of Winnipeg would emerge.

Archibald MacDonald did not return to Scotland. He joined the Hudson's Bay Company and was soon identified as a man of considerable ability by George Simpson, another Scot and governor of the vast territory presided over by the HBC. In 1821, the year that the HBC merged with the North West Company, MacDonald was posted to Oregon Territory, and 18 years later his nephew Angus was at Fort Colvile. Family connections and personal recommendations helped. A striking example of the Scots' reliance on networking is the MacTavish family. Simon MacTavish recruited numerous extended family members to the North West Company, and ensured that he himself was succeeded by a nephew, William MacGillivray. It may have been nepotism, but it was effective. There was too much at stake to risk appointing lightweights or men beyond the influence of blood connection.

The MacDonald family, who left a deep imprint on trade and settlement on both sides of the border (Mt MacDonald in Montana is named for Angus), helps to illustrate why so many Scots, Highlanders in particular, were prominent in this chapter of the American frontier story. The North West Company, founded in 1779, and the much older Hudson's Bay Company recruited hundreds of Highlanders and Orkneymen, as they were considered suitable material for the demands of the wilderness. They were tough and resourceful, often used to hardship and certainly acquainted with harsh landscapes and demanding conditions. 'We were poor and had to get through life in the hardest manner,' wrote Robert

Stuart's sister-in-law. In spite of poverty, Robert was educated to a level that enabled him to start his working life as a schoolteacher.

There was fierce competition for employment with both fur-trading companies as they were seen as a route out of dead-end Highland poverty. In the second half of the 18th century the erosion of the clan system, accelerated by the collapse of the Jacobite movement after the 1746 defeat at Culloden, had a devastating economic effect on the Highlands, and throughout the 19th century communities struggled to survive. Their young men often had little choice but to leave. Their most likely options were to join the army or to go to North America; often the former led to the latter. Many of those taken on by the fur trade started their careers as clerks. Robert Stuart is an example. It is a job he could not have done if he had not been both literate and numerate. This was an advantage Scots generally had over the thousands of European emigrants flooding into North America in the 19th century.

Although the Astorian venture was aborted, fur trapping and trading in the northwest continued and increased. New American companies were formed and competition with the British companies intensified. Robert Stuart and Ramsay Crooks started their own fur-trading business, and then in 1816 both joined the American Fur Company. Stuart was based on Mackinac Island until in 1834 he went to Detroit. He became Michigan's state treasurer and secretary of the Illinois Canal Company. He was also federal superintendent of Indian affairs. He was joined both in Mackinac and Detroit by his Uncle David. Crooks went on to become president of the American Fur Company, and died in 1859 in New York City. By that time the trail that he and Stuart had blazed through the Rocky Mountains from west to east was deeply rutted by the thousands of wagons that had headed east to west.

Two works of fiction by an author of Scottish descent chronicle both the era of the mountain men and the wagon-train pioneers who followed them. A.B. Guthrie's *The Big Sky* (1947) draws on contemporary accounts to convey a memorable and authentic narrative of the fur trade, which rapidly became a classic of Western literature. The 1952 movie version was directed by Howard Hawks and starred Kirk Douglas. *The Big Sky* captures the loneliness and hardship of long months in the mountains, but also the freedom:

> This was the way to live, free and easy, with time all a man's own and none to say no to him. A body got so's he felt everything was kin to him, the earth and sky and buffalo and beaver and the yellow moon at night. It was better than being walled in by a house...

The sequel, *The Way West* (1949), describes the legacy of the mountain men and signals the inevitable end, which is already foreseen by *The Big Sky*'s mountain heroes Boone Caudill and Dick Summers. Boone imagines 'churches and courthouses and such standing where he used to stand alone'. But 20 years would pass before other than mountain men and fur traders would make the journey that Guthrie celebrates. More Scots were involved in blazing the trails that made the trans-continental trek possible. Robert Campbell, an Ulster Scot who arrived in America in 1824, joined with William Sublette to form a fur-trading company, trapped with famed mountain men and trail guides Tom Fitzpatrick and Jim Bridger, and later became an Indian commissioner. He died a rich man in 1879.

If the Scottish mountain men have never quite become the stuff of legend, another trailblazer and Indian scout of Scottish descent unequivocally has. Kit Carson's great-grandfather, Alexander Carson, was a Presbyterian minister in Dumfriesshire, and emigrated to Pennsylvania by way of Ulster. His son William moved on to North Carolina, and *his* son to Kentucky, where Christopher was born in 1809, and then to Missouri, illustrating a common pattern of movement west. Many Scots and Ulster Scots were among the first to cross the Alleghenies in the 18th century and to move the frontier west.

At the age of 15 Kit became apprenticed to a saddle maker. Two years later he'd had enough, and headed west. The self-sufficiency and toughness bred by the back country often made it difficult to settle down, and the ever-shifting frontier beckoned. For 18 years Kit Carson survived as fur trapper and mountain man, working for a time in Idaho for the Hudson's Bay Company. But by the 1830s the fur trade was in decline, and the last rendezvous, the annual gathering of trappers to sell on their furs, took place on the Green River in 1840. In 1842 Carson was taken on as guide and scout by the explorer John Charles Frémont. It was the start of a long and eventful career as scout, soldier and Indian agent.

Frémont described Carson as 'a man of medium height, broad-shouldered and deep-chested, with a clear steady blue eye and frank speech and address; quiet and unassuming'. He was also, contrary to Scottish tradition, illiterate. Frémont's objective was to explore officially areas which up to then were known only to Native Americans and mountain men, whose experience of the terrain was rarely set down on paper. In particular, it was hoped that he would locate connecting waterways that would lead to the Pacific. What he established was that such a passage did not exist. If people and goods were going to cross the continent, they were going to have to find suitable overland routes. By this time, the impetus from increasing numbers looking to head west was such that the deserts and mountains that stood in their way were not going to continue as barriers for much longer.

In 1823 Stephen H. Long published a map based on his expedition of 1819–20, which described a vast area east of the Rockies as the 'Great American Desert'. In his view, the scarcity of water meant that it was 'almost wholly unfit for cultivation, and of course, uninhabitable by a people depending upon agriculture for their subsistence'. It would, he said, 'prove an insuperable obstacle in the way of settling the country'. An 1843 article in the *Edinburgh Review* described the territory between the United States and Oregon as 'a howling wilderness of snow and tempests' for half the year and an area of 'hopeless sterility' for the other half. It was also infested with savage Indians 'who cannot be tracked, overtaken, or conciliated'. John Dunn of the Hudson's Bay Company believed that 'there is no secure, expeditious, or commodious tract which can ever be used as a highway, so as to afford facilities for an influx of emigrants over-land'. They were wrong. Whatever the obstacles, and they were very real, those aiming for the fertile valleys on the far side of the Rocky Mountains were not to be deterred, and Kit Carson was one of those who helped them to get there.

Carson proved himself in many ways. With Frémont he was drawn into the struggle with Mexico for control of California, and was sent by Frémont with dispatches overland to Washington. It took him a couple of months to make a journey similar to the one that 30 years earlier had taken Robert Stuart a year. By the end of the 1840s thousands were crossing the deserts and mountains, lured to endure often appalling hardship by the prospect of fertile land and then by gold, discovered in California in 1848. The forts established by the fur trade found an additional role more or less imposed on them, and new supply posts sprang up to service the emigrants. Entrepreneurs were quick to exploit the needs of the wagon trains undeterred by the pessimists. There were plenty of emigrants who didn't make it, and plenty who turned back, but the flow was now unstoppable. Equally unstoppable were those who saw an opportunity to adapt from the fur trade to the wagon train.

Fort Hall on the Snake River (in present-day Idaho) was a Hudson's Bay Company post opened in 1834. Richard Grant had been with the company for 21 years when he was appointed its commandant in 1842. He was under specific orders not to assist emigrants aiming for Oregon, and believed himself that the route northwest from Fort Hall was not possible by wagon. Fort Hall was positioned near to where the trail divided, north to Oregon, south to California. Grant encouraged emigrants instead to aim for California, and provided them with maps, guides and provisions at favourable prices. He soon gained a reputation for his helpfulness to travellers.

There was increasing pressure for the United States to take over Oregon and bring an end to British activities in the territory. An influx of American settlers could only strengthen the US foothold. Nevertheless, Grant was one of many Scots whose fur trade knowledge of the northwest opened the way for settlement even as they resisted it. He successfully made the transition from trailblazer to enabler, and overlanders would have cause to be grateful. Over the next few years, in spite of numerous disasters and setbacks, the current of emigration increased exponentially. When in 1846 the British renounced their claim to Oregon, the Hudson's Bay Company withdrew north. But Scots continued to be part of the Oregon story, as pioneer settlers and farmers. John McLoughlin in 1842 founded Oregon City on the Willamette River, which became a destination for many pioneers and a focus of settlement. It was 30 years after Robert Stuart had first recognised the attractions of the Willamette Valley.

CHAPTER 2

Texas

I woke up one morning on the old Chisholm Trail,
Rope in my hand and a cow by the tail.

'The Old Chisholm Trail', traditional

ON 6 MARCH 1836 Mexican troops commanded by General Santa Anna attacked the Alamo in San Antonio, Texas. The adobe walls of what had once been a Spanish mission were being defended by 180 men. Among them was John Macgregor, who played the bagpipes as Santa Anna unleashed a furious assault. It is reckoned that about a third of the defenders were of Scottish origins, including the famed Davy Crockett and Jim Bowie.

Texan volunteers had occupied the half-ruined Alamo three months earlier, after an opportunistic expedition to take San Antonio. The situation in Texas, then part of Mexico, was volatile, after decades of contention between Spain and the US. Since the Louisiana Purchase in 1803, when Jefferson vastly increased US territory, there had been controversy on the Mexican border. The Spanish had been the first Europeans in Texas, establishing missions and forts and small communities. But from around 1815 Anglo-Americans were filtering into the territory, attracted by cheap land. By 1830 there were 10,000 Americans in Texas – squatters, Indian traders, speculators, and criminals and misfits who were more comfortable beyond the reach of US law. Many of the incomers were from the southern states, and brought their slaves with them.

There were clashes with the Mexican population and with the Mexican government, which itself experienced a series of upheavals. A rebellion against Royalist Spanish rule led in 1833 to Santa Anna being elected president of Mexico. The Mexican grip on Texas was tightening, but at the same time Americans were crossing the Rio Grande looking for land. One of them was Dr James Grant, who had acquired landholdings in Coahuila south of the river. He had a vested interest in extending the American presence, and was a prominent 'hawk' when it came to talk of war. He was one of many Scottish players in the events of 1835–6.

In 1828 a young man called Samuel Houston was elected governor of Tennessee. He had already had a colourful career. His family were Ulster Scots who settled first in Virginia and then, like so many others, moved on to Tennessee. As a teenager he left his widowed mother and frontier home to live with the Cherokee, and in 1814 fought against the Creeks under General Andrew Jackson at Horseshoe Bend. The wounds he received caused him problems for the rest of his life. He became Indian Agent to the Cherokee, then studied law and moved into politics, and was elected to Congress in 1823. It helped that he received the support of Andrew Jackson, now resident in the White House.

Sam Houston's departure from Tennessee and a conventional political role was sudden. In 1829 his recent marriage collapsed and he resigned as governor. After a spell back with the Cherokee, Houston found himself drawn into the events unfolding in Texas. President Jackson wanted Texas as part of the USA, which was why no serious efforts were made to restrain the activities of freebooters like James Grant. Sam Houston was physically impressive, a military hero, politically experienced, intelligent, a skilled frontiersman and a strong personality. Jackson identified him as just the man to send into Texas. Houston set off, crossing the Red River, which divides Texas from what is now Arkansas and Oklahoma, in December 1832. He would become what Dale Van Every has described as 'the George Washington of the Texas Revolution'.

He settled in Nacogdoches, near the border with Louisiana, a typically lawless frontier town that offered him plenty of scope to practise his professional skills. In his view, as Americans continued to cross into Texas, it would only be a matter of time before the territory declared its independence as a first step towards joining the USA, but there were hotheads (like Grant) who did not want to wait. There were several small-scale skirmishes and clashes.

The situation came to the boil towards the end of 1835. Increasing numbers of Americans were volunteering to fight for an American Texas. In November, the Texas convention declared Texas an autonomous republic, and Houston was appointed commander-in-chief of the forces. Opinion was divided as to the best course of action. There was no single political focus, and there were bands of volunteers, often inexperienced, untrained and undisciplined, looking for a role. It was all highly combustible.

At the end of 1835 came the surrender of the Mexican army occupying San Antonio, which had been under siege by the Americans for some time. There were those who thought the war was won, and many of the volunteers went back to their neglected homesteads. There were some who agitated for more aggressive action. James Grant wanted to invade Mexico, hoping to regain his Coahuila land. This was just one example of personal interests undermining the authority of Houston, who was finding it hard to control what had never been a real army. Then came the news that Santa Anna had crossed the Rio Grande and was heading for San Antonio. Houston despatched another band of volunteers, led by William Travis, to defend the town. Travis occupied the Alamo and sent out urgent pleas for help. They withstood 12 days of attack before they all died.

In joint command at the Alamo was James Bowie, a Scottish American from a Tennessee family. Known best for his frontier prowess and his reputed invention of the bowie knife, he was also an educated and cultured man who spoke several languages fluently and was well liked. He drifted into Texas in search of adventure, like so many others, and got involved in land speculation, became a Mexican citizen and married Ursula de Veramendi, the daughter of the Mexican vice-governor.

Davy Crockett arrived at the Alamo a few days after Travis, with another band of volunteers. His origins were also in Scotland

and Tennessee, the nursery of so many who made their mark on the moving frontier. His father was killed at King's Mountain during the Revolutionary War, a battle in which each side, Patriot and Loyalist, was led by a Scot. Like Sam Houston, Davy Crockett fought under Andrew Jackson against the Creeks at Horseshoe Bend and went on to a political career, but unlike Houston he clashed with Jackson during his three terms in Congress, which led to his ultimate defeat. Crockett was a flamboyant personality who presented himself as a bluff frontiersman, and he was as well known for his story-telling as he was for his marksmanship. When at the age of 49 his political career collapsed he went west, and once in Texas it was almost inevitable that he would become involved in the rebellion. If he was not already an iconic figure, the legendary defence of the Alamo made him one.

In March 1836, Texas declared independence and elected David Burnet as provisional president. Burnet was critical of Houston, whom he felt was dragging his feet as army commander while Santa Anna swept onwards. But Houston was having to rebuild his own forces, whose numbers fluctuated as settler volunteers balanced the needs of their homesteads and families. The new Texas government took fright and headed for Galveston, with Santa Anna in pursuit, reck-lessly as it turned out, for Houston was now in a position to stalk the pursuers. On 21 April he surprised the Mexican army near the mouth of the San Jacinto River, near the present-day city of Houston. Before he attacked he addressed his men: 'Some of us may be killed and must be killed, but soldiers, remember the Alamo!' Victory came quickly. There were 630 Mexican fatalities, and eight American. Houston's horse was killed, and he himself was wounded. Santa Anna was captured. A decade of Texan independence was assured.

Sam Houston's subsequent career was mixed. Texas was in chaos and he required urgent medical treatment, but in September he was elected president of Texas. There were at this time around 30,000 'Anglo-Americans' in Texas, and around 5,000 black slaves, 3,500

Mexicans and 14,500 Native Americans. With his background and long involvement with the Cherokee, Houston was keen to establish fair treatment for the mainly Apache and Comanche people, but the Texas senate did not support him. When Houston's first term as president came to an end, an anti-Indian policy dominated. A key figure in negotiations with the Comanche was Hugh McLeod, a West Point graduate who was one of two Texas commissioners. An ill-managed attempt to persuade the Comanche to hand over white captives resulted in fighting, which left 35 Comanche dead. Their chief, Buffalo Hump, led a revenge raid on Victoria on the Guadalupe River, killing settlers and stealing livestock. They were pursued north to Plum Creek near Lockhart by a group of volunteers, one of whose leaders was a man called Ben McCulloch, who would play a key role in the activities of the Texas Rangers. (Lockhart is also a Scottish name; one of Buffalo Hump's captives was a young girl called Matilda Lockhart.) In 1841 Houston had a second term as president, and was governor of Texas from 1859 to 1861, but his formative years with the Cherokee cut little ice with the growing number of settlers, among them of course many Scots, who saw Indians as a threat to a secure future.

The frontiers with Mexico and with Indian country remained problematic for many years. Before Texas was admitted to the Union in 1845 there were frequent clashes, and then in 1846 all-out war with Mexico, egged on by those who believed that it was part of the 'manifest destiny' of the United States to absorb California, Arizona, Nevada and New Mexico. Scots played their part in these turbulent years, as settlers and administrators, fighters and freebooters. The names of the state's towns and counties reflect the Scottish presence: Houston, of course, but also Edinburgh, Dallas, Guthrie, McLean, Baird, Rankin, Hamilton, McAllen, Cameron, Caldwell, Anderson, Armstrong, Gillespie, McCulloch, Robertson, Henderson, Graham and numerous others. They represent not just Scots, but also specific individuals who made a contribution to the development of Texas.

With the admission of Texas to the Union and the resolution of the Mexican War with the Treaty of Guadalupe in 1848, settlement increased, but it was still a risky business. Most settlers were living off the land, trying to make a success of farming or ranching, but in addition to the practical challenges, a fluid border and resistant Indians were threats to stability. Forts were built along the lower Rio Grande to protect the border – Forts McIntosh and Duncan indicating a Scottish origin. In September 1850, a band of 117 intending English and Scottish settlers led by Highlander Lieutenant Charles F. Mackenzie, was heading for Texas, 'pioneers in a great and glorious enterprise', in the words of *The Messenger* newspaper. The group included merchants, ironmongers, tailors, butchers and bakers, from Lancashire, the Midlands, and Glasgow and Edinburgh. They sailed from Liverpool to Galveston, and then made their way to Cow House Creek, 65 miles north of Austin, to establish a colony called New Britain. But the site turned out to be hilly and stony, and quite unsuitable for the city they planned to build. Most of the band headed further east to Cameron, where some were able to buy land, but others gave up on Texas altogether and went to New Orleans. Eventually, 27,000 acres were purchased along the Brazos River north of Waco. Each settler got 20 acres. But there were crop failures and Comanche raids, and within a year that too had been abandoned. The realities of settlement were overlaid by the realities of heroic endeavour.

This was not a success story, but frontier conditions could breed a response to potential danger that relied on both individual and collective action. It has been pointed out that the background of Scottish Highlanders and Borderers in particular made them especially suited to frontier life. The Scottish Borders are also a frontier, for many centuries a disputed and difficult to govern territory with a tradition of lawlessness and conflict. The Highlands had similar traditions of fierce clan loyalties and enmities, in a landscape that demanded a tough self-sufficiency. The rugged independence associated with the American frontier was part of the Scottish inheritance, and almost certainly contributed more than a little to the American frontier ethos.

Although the realities of settlement could be masked by the evocation of heroic endeavour, there were plenty of examples of the latter and of Scottish input to intrepid action. Several Scots joined the Texas Rangers, whose origins go back to 1823, when Stephen Austin, one of the first Anglo-Americans to promote organised settlement in Texas, got together 10 men to protect against Indian raids. Their leader was Captain James Ross. By 1835 there existed an irregular band of fighters known as the Texas Rangers, and the following year the new government of Texas passed a law requiring the president to raise a militia of 280 men, each to provide their own horse, rifle and brace of pistols. Scottish names are prominent: Colonel Bain, Captain Cunningham, General Douglas, Captain Caldwell, Captain Cameron, and perhaps above all the brothers Ben and Henry McCulloch.

The McCullochs were born in Tennessee, neighbours of Davy Crockett whom they followed to Texas. Ben McCulloch joined the volunteers fighting for Texan independence and commanded the artillery at the Battle of San Jacinto. After the war he settled in Gonzales, on the Guadalupe River between Houston and San Antonio. McCulloch became renowned for his courage and his frontier skills. The frontier historian Walter Prescott Webb described him:

> A man of bold features, prominent forehead, straight nose, and deep-set blue eyes... His face a mask and his features under such control as to give no clue as to his feelings, or emotions, or intentions, it was as natural for Ben McCulloch to remain calm in danger as it was to breathe. Sudden emergencies served to quicken his faculties, rather than to confuse them. His courage may best be described as a complete absence of fear.

Another Texas historian, Randolph B. Campbell, quotes an anonymous trooper who provided a vivid collective picture of the Rangers:

A more reckless, devil-may-care looking set, it would be impossible to find this side of the Infernal Regions. Take them altogether, with their uncouth costumes, bearded faces, lean and brawny forms, fierce wild eyes and swaggering manners, they were fit representatives of the outlaws which made up the population of the Lone Star State.

To the Mexicans they were known as *'los Tejanos diablos'*. To General Taylor, under whom McCulloch and his men worked as scouts during the Mexican War, they were 'the damndest troops in the world', and he went on, 'We can't do without them in a fight, and we can't do anything with them out of a fight.' A band of Rangers under Richard Gillespie also served under General Taylor. Henry McCulloch, Ben's brother, commanded the First Texas Mounted Rifles, created as a defence against Comanche raids.

By the 1880s, the Rangers' task was law enforcement rather than Indian fighting. Plenty of Scottish names continued to feature. In his book *The West that Was, from Texas to Montana* (1958), John Leakey gives an account of a Ranger called P.C. Baird who in 1884 was investigating cattle rustling and clashes between ranchers and sheep farmers. Leakey's account has its comic moments:

> [the Rangers] stood up and pulled their guns, ready to go into action and demand the 'rustlers' surrender. But, strangely, they hadn't checked their guns and ammunition until that moment – when they were mortified to discover that they had taken too many pot shots at rattlesnakes on the way over the day before, thereby running themselves dangerously short on ammunition.

In the shoot-out that followed one of the four rustlers was killed and a Ranger wounded. The three remaining rustlers dashed for their horses and got away. Leakey reports without comment that 'Baird wrote that he could easily have shot all the horses, but that he was so short of ammunition he preferred to let them get away'.

One of the most notable Texas Rangers at the end of the century was Captain Bill McDonald. He is portrayed by Walter Prescott Webb as the epitome of the Western hero:

> To his other gifts Bill added a good fighting Scotch name, a fine face lined with sun, wind, and character, a pair of mild blue eyes, and a soft voice, and a 'suddenness' – things that made him irresistible to friend or enemy... The philosophy that supported him, and had supported all the great Rangers before him, Bill McDonald articulated in striking phrases: 'No man in the wrong can stand up against a fellow that's in the right and keeps on a-comin'.

But he seems also to have been able to defuse potential violence with calm persuasion.

In his *Lonesome Dove* series of novels Larry McMurtry portrays the life of the Texas Rangers in the 1850s and 1860s. His characters are a ragbag of misfits and drop-outs, reflecting the anarchy of the moving frontier and echoing the lives of figures such as the McCullochs, Davy Crockett and Kit Carson. Some are experienced trackers and Indian scouts; some stumble into Texas as raw youths who have hardly handled a rifle. They are restless, starved of the company of women, and often scared. They operate in a harsh land against a relentless enemy, represented most threateningly by Buffalo Hump, the Comanche chief Ben McCulloch helped to defeat at Plum Creek. The central characters in the McMurtry novels are Gus McCrae from Tennessee, and Woodrow Coll, who acknowledges his Scottish ancestry. The owners of the Austin general store are called Forsythe. Another with a Scottish name is Bigfoot Wallace, based on W.A.A. 'Big Foot' Wallace who in 1837 drifted into Texas from Virginia at the age of 20. After a spell as a Ranger, he was stage driver on the route from Austin to El Paso, 700 miles through difficult terrain with a risk of Indian attack. McMurtry depicts Bigfoot as 'the most respected scout on the Texas frontier', a determined tracker and an authority on Native customs and the best way to forestall capture and possible torture by the Comanche – with a self-inflicted bullet through the eyeball.

McMurtry's novels are Western adventure stories with a vein of comedy, but his evocation of an unforgiving land, the struggle of ordinary people to survive and build communities, and the multi-ethnic collection of men and women who tried to make the territory a safer if not a more civilised place is vivid and convincing. The threat is impersonated in the sinister, silent figure of Buffalo Hump, who features prominently in Texas history. Lawrence Sullivan Ross was the son of a subagent on the Brazos reservation, who led raids against him, and may be the inspiration for McMurtry's fictional accounts. In an attack on Buffalo Hump's village near Fort Arbuckle, Ross was badly wounded. He captained a mixed band of volunteers and soldiers in a raid on Comanche camped on Pease River, and recovered Cynthia Ann Parker who had been taken captive many years before. She had married a Comanche chief and borne three children, one of whom, Quanah, would become one of the best-remembered Comanche chiefs. Sol Ross, as he was known, fought in the Civil War, and in 1887 became governor of Texas.

Texas was still very volatile when the Civil War erupted in 1861. With so many southern slave owners among its settlers – 30 per cent of the state's population of over 600,000 were slaves – it was no surprise that Texas voted to secede with the other southern states, in spite of Sam Houston's efforts to dissuade the convention. Texas troops were prominent at Shiloh, where the Confederates were defeated, and at Chickamauga and Glorieta, which were Confederate victories. Ben McCulloch was quick to join up and in 1861 his troops defeated a Union force at Wilson's Creek, Missouri, and occupied Springfield. The following year he was killed at Elkhorn Tavern, Arkansas, along with his second-in-command, James McIntosh.

With the end of the Civil War, the numbers crossing into Texas increased, a consequence of the upheavals that came in the wake of war and of peace. There was an influx particularly from the southern states, people abandoning devastation and the struggle to adjust to a changing political and social environment. The prospect of a new life in a pioneer state was tempting. But there were still dangers. Expanding settlement was a threat to the Kiowa, Comanche and Apache people who saw their territory shrinking. They struck back. A series of campaigns attempted to contain or remove them. In 1871 Colonel Ranald Mackenzie, a Raasay born West Point graduate and Civil War veteran (in which he had lost a finger – the Comanche called him 'Three Fingers'), took command of the 4th United States cavalry, based at Fort Richardson on the West Fork of the Trinity River. Mackenzie was known for his cunning as well as his shortness of temper. He campaigned in the Llano Estacado, the unforgiving Staked Plains towards the New Mexico border, which feature in many Westerns (including McMurtry's), and then along the Rio Grande. In September 1872, Mackenzie raided a Comanche village camped on McClellan's Creek in the upper reaches of the Red River. The lodges were destroyed, 23 Comanche killed, and the women and children captured. Most of the Comanche herd of horses, over a thousand, were also captured. Without their horses, the Comanche were severely weakened.

Official American policy was to contain the tribes in reservations, which of course put an end to their nomadic way of life and most of the activities that were at the heart of their culture. One of the most resistant chiefs was Cynthia Ann Parker's son Quanah, who in 1874 led a band of Kiowa, Comanche and Southern Cheyenne in a raid on a buffalo-hunters' camp at Adobe Walls on the Canadian River. The hunters were believed to have stolen Indian horses, but more of a threat to the Comanche way of life and that of many other tribes was the slaughter by white men of their prime source of food. Although Quanah and his men inflicted significant damage at Adobe Walls, they suffered many casualties, and withdrew. In reprisal Colonel Mackenzie, with the help of Apache scouts, tracked them down to their village hidden deep in Palo Duro canyon near the New Mexico border. It was autumn, and the Comanche and their allies the Kiowa were preparing for winter, gathering food supplies. Mackenzie's men attacked, burning lodges and destroying provisions. Over a thousand horses were captured and killed. Many

Indians escaped, without horses, clothing and food, but were systematically hunted down and captured. Eventually, Quanah Parker and over 400 of his followers surrendered at Fort Sill in Indian Territory (now Oklahoma). It marked the end of the Comanche threat. It would be another few years before the Apaches finally gave up their struggle, and Mackenzie had a role in that too.

In the northwest corner of Texas lies the Panhandle, at first not considered suitable for settlement, partly because it was so susceptible to Indian attack. It would become the focus of a phenomenon in which Scots played a major part: the cattle bonanza. Ranching in Texas and Mexico had been well established for decades, and the skills and appurtenances that we think of as characteristic of the American cowboy originated with the Spanish, who had introduced cattle to the New World. In the chaos of the Civil War years and their aftermath opportunistic cattlemen were rounding up wild or unbranded cattle and selling them to a market greedy for beef. According to Edgar Bronson, who embarked on his career as a cattleman in 1872, 'all the best punchers were Texans', often ex-Confederate soldiers or their sons.

When the war was over, the challenge of how to get the beasts to market intensified, whether it was to the west, where the Colorado gold rush was attracting thousands, or to the east, where a growing population needed meat. Trailing cattle long distances was a hazardous business, but it was the only way to move them. In 1864 an enterprising man called Jesse Chisholm, part Cherokee, part Scottish, took a wagon train of goods from Wichita in Kansas through Indian Territory to Texas. Nearly 90 years earlier his grandfather John Chisholm had arrived from Scotland, and his son Ignatius, Jesse's father, married the daughter of a Cherokee chief. (The links between Scots and the Cherokee are particularly strong.) In the spring following his trip south Jesse headed back along the same trail with buffalo hides and cattle. Within another year it was established as the Chisholm Trail, a vital link in connecting Texas cattle with markets in the east.

The other vital link was the railroad. The progress of railroad building west of the Mississippi had been interrupted by the war, but by 1867 the Kansas Pacific Railroad was moving west, with small towns springing up along the track. A man called Joseph McCoy was concerned about the dearth of cattle reaching Kansas City and Chicago for slaughter. He decided to take action, and set his sights on a little place called Abilene. He recognised the potential of what he described as 'a very small, dead place consisting of about one dozen log huts, low, small, rude affairs; four-fifths of which were covered with dirt for roofing'. Such business as was conducted in the town took place in two of the log huts. Another hut was the saloon.

McCoy bought land and built stockyards and pens, a barn, an office and a hotel. He sent out circulars and advertised in the Chicago press: the challenge was to get not only the cattle to Abilene, but the buyers also. In the first year 36,000 cattle were shipped out of Abilene, having been trailed up from Texas. By 1869 the number had reached 100,000; the following year it was 300,000. By then, 1870, there were 10 boarding houses, 10 saloons, five general stores and four hotels. There were plenty of outlets for end-of-trail-happy cowboys to spend their wages.

The trail drives averaged 15 miles a day, over rough country. Many of the cattle originated in southern Texas, some in Mexico. There were several major rivers and numerous smaller streams to cross, with the Brazos and the Red being especially difficult. Sometimes cattle and cowboys drowned. There could be Indian attacks, and there was always the risk of stampedes, which could also result in fatalities. It is no surprise that Scottish names appear in the early years of the post-Civil War cattle business, and they would become even more familiar in the late 1870s and 1880s. Scotland's tradition of cattle-raising, cattle-droving and cattle-thieving went back many centuries. Highlanders and Borderers in particular were good at all these activities, and numbers of them, or their descendants, found themselves in Texas after the war. The connection can be traced in cowboy folklore and music also. As one of the earliest collectors of cowboy songs, John A. Lomax, remarked cowboy songs preserved the 'ballad spirit' of the remoter areas of Scotland and England.

> Illiterate people, and people cut off from newspapers and books, isolated and lonely folk... express themselves through somewhat the same character of songs as did their forefathers of perhaps a thousand years ago.

And the line of connection between Scotland's Border ballads and Western ballads is direct, sustained as it was through succeeding generations of Scottish Americans who moved through the Appalachians and on from Kentucky and Tennessee, and who left their musical imprint on Bluegrass and country music as they went.

One of the best-known cowboy songs is 'The Old Chisholm Trail', which details the life of a cowboy on his 'ten-dollar horse' with 'a forty-dollar saddle':

> *I woke up one morning on the old Chisholm Trail,*
> *Rope in my hand and a cow by the tail.*

There follows a saga of endless work, foul weather, stampedes, a diet of bacon and beans, and measly pay, until finally:

> *I'll sell my horse and I'll sell my saddle;*
> *You can go to hell with your longhorn cattle.*

There are many versions of this song, but the general drift is the same: the cowpuncher's life was not an easy one.

The railroad moved west and so did the destinations of the cattle herds. Ellsworth, Hays City, Dodge City, each took their turn and each had their cast of legendary characters, cowboys, sheriffs, outlaws, saloon managers, brothel keepers, as well as ordinary folk who gradually shaped a 'respectable' community. Scots had a share in all these roles. In Texas itself communities gradually became more stable. Scots could be found anywhere in the state, and were particularly conspicuous in the Hill Country near Austin and in the Panhandle. With the boom in beef many Scots put money into Texas cattle or came to the state as ranch managers.

More than anything, Texas needed a population. It needed people to secure the frontier, and it needed particular skills to develop its resources. Scots had a reputation all over the US for their abilities as farmers and gardeners, and as miners, quarrymen and textile workers. In 1867, a firm in Houston recruited 18 Highlanders to work as ploughmen on Texas farms. In 1886, masons from Aberdeen were brought to Austin to cut stone used for building the state capitol. They hadn't realised when they were recruited that they were to be used as strike breakers, which meant they were blacklisted by the American union. Used to working in north east Scotland, they found the punishing Texas heat hard to endure: three did not survive it.

The railroads made it easier to move people as well as cattle, and it was in the railroad companies' interests to attract settlers. Company brochures were distributed in Scotland. One brochure for the Texas Central Railway advertises 5,000,000 acres of land, 'not only suitable for Agricultural purposes but also for raising Cattle' in what is described as 'the Garden of Eden of America'. One of the Texas officials featured on the brochure is Robert M. Elgin, a Scottish name. Scottish involvement in the administrative and political life of Texas did not come to an end with Sam Houston. There is a particular concentration of Scottish names among state governors and other prominent politicians in the late 19th and early 20th century: James Hogg, Thomas Campbell, William McLean, James Ferguson. The latter distinguished himself by becoming the only Texas governor to be impeached, for embezzlement and the misuse of public funds. He was convicted. But when in office he espoused the problems of small tenant farmers and sharecroppers, and provided more money for rural schools and roads.

In the last decades of the 20th century the links between Scotland and Texas were revived when Scotland was developing its own oil industry. Texas had been producing oil since the 1920s, when drilling began in the Panhandle, and Texas oil expertise came to Scotland. It was a new kind of frontier; most of those concerned probably did not reflect on how Scots had played a part – and often led the way – on the Texas frontier.

CHAPTER 3

Securing the Frontier

We'll first chastise, then civilise, bold Johnny Navajo.

Composed by one of Kit Carson's men

IN 1850 COLONEL GEORGE MCCALL inspected military outposts in New Mexico, which was beginning to attract settlement and trade. It was Apache country. In Colonel McCall's view, no accommodation could be made with the Jicarilla Apaches, who would 'continue to rob and murder our citizens until they are exterminated'. When Apaches attacked a Santa Fé trader called James White and his family, Kit Carson joined the hunt to recover the women who had been carried off. He found Mrs White with an arrow through her, and a book in which he himself featured as a frontier hero. The Whites' daughter and a black servant were never found.

Government efforts to persuade Native Americans into reservations and to adapt to the life imported by white settlement were slow to take effect. Few believed that anything but military force could bring the tribes to give up their traditional ways of life. But reservations were expensive and difficult to run. Deprived of the freedom to hunt and sustain themselves, Indians had to be fed and clothed. James Calhoun, Superintendent of Indian Affairs in New Mexico, made his views clear: 'To establish order in this territory, you must either submit to these heavy expenditures, or exterminate the mass of these Indians.' There were plenty of people who favoured extermination over expense.

Kit Carson wasn't one of them. In 1853 he was appointed agent for the Muache Utes, and made his base in Taos. He was in favour of reservations, and felt that Indians should be helped towards self-sufficiency, which meant they had to learn to farm.

Nomadic hunter-gatherer people like the Apache were profoundly resistant. The process of persuading them and other tribes, often with violence but sometimes more peaceably, involved a significant number of Scots.

With the outbreak of the Civil War, Carson resigned as agent and joined the New Mexico Volunteer Indian Regiment, becoming colonel despite his lack of formal military training. He took part in only one engagement against the Confederates, at Valverde. The rest of the time he was occupied in campaigns against Apaches and Navajos. It was Carson who in January 1864 led the expedition into Canyon de Chelly in north eastern Arizona – one of the most memorable pictures taken by the iconic photographer of the West, Edward Curtis, depicts it – that resulted in Navajo capitulation. It inspired the following verse from one of the men:

> *Come dress your ranks, my gallant souls, and standing in a row,*
> *Kit Carson he is waiting to march upon the foe;*
> *At night we march to Moqui, o'er lofty hills of snow,*
> *To meet and crush the savage foe, bold Johnny Navajo.*
> *Johnny Navajo! O Johnny Navajo!*
> *We'll first chastise, then civilise, bold Johnny Navajo.*

The Navajo were already weakened by a hard winter and lack of food. Carson destroyed their crops. In March, the 2,400 men, women and children who had surrendered set off on the never-forgotten Long Walk of 300 miles to the reservation at Bosque Redondo, near Fort Sumner on the Pecos River. Later, several thousand more were sent to join them, about 11,500 in all. Nearly 3,000 of them never made it. The extreme cold, hunger, dysentery and heartbreak at the loss of their land took their toll. Some escaped. Some of the children were stolen to be sold on as labour.

In his report on the operation Kit Carson stated that the Navajo had been shown that 'in no place, however formidable or inaccessible, are they safe from the pursuit of troops of this command'. He added that he had convinced many of them that government intentions towards them were 'eminently humane; and dictated by an earnest desire to promote their welfare; that the principle is not to destroy but to save them, if they are disposed to be saved'. But the Navajo had a wretched few years struggling to survive at Bosque Redondo where alkali soil and brackish water made farming almost impossible. In 1868 they were allowed to return to their own country.

Kit Carson's sympathy for Native Americans was genuine, and he tried to insist that they be treated with fairness. But equally he accepted as right and inevitable that white settlement should prevail. One after another, the trans-Missouri territories were added to the Union: Kansas in 1861, Nevada in 1864, Nebraska in 1867, Colorado in 1876. Carson died in 1868, when the Indian wars were moving into their final phase. A key figure in that final phase was General George Crook, born in 1828 in Ohio, of Scottish descent. He served in the Civil War and then for six years in Idaho, before taking on the Apache in Arizona. Crook was a tall, imposing, bearded figure, who soon established a reputation for being firm but fair-minded. The Apache people knew him as 'Gray Wolf'. John Bourke, who served with him, described him as 'a clear-headed thinker, a fluent conversationalist, and a most pleasant companion'. He frequently emphasised his energy, intelligence and patience.

In the winter of 1871 a small band of Aravaipa Apache arrived at Camp Grant on Arizona's San Pedro River and asked permission to camp nearby. This was allowed, on condition that they gave up their weapons, which they did. They settled a few miles away and got on with their lives; some were employed by the troops based at Camp Grant and by local ranchers. Relations were good, and more Apache joined them. Over 50 miles away in Tucson things were not so relaxed. In April there were two Apache raids nearby, and the mixed citizenry of Tucson – miners, traders and the usual frontier hangers-on – decided to take matters into their own hands. A band of 140 armed volunteers set out for the Apache village near Camp

Grant. Unarmed and totally taken by surprise, over a hundred Apache, mainly women and children, were slaughtered.

At Camp Grant at the time was Scottish American Andrew Cargill. He accompanied Lieutenant Whitman, who as soon as he heard news of the Tucson raiders rode straight for the Apache village. They were too late. Surveying the carnage, Cargill commented: 'We knew at once it had been done by parties from Tucson.' Lieutenant Whitman was determined to bring the perpetrators to trial, and when he eventually succeeded Andrew Cargill was secretary to the grand jury. But in spite of the evidence and witnesses who swore that the Aravaipa village was a peaceful settlement, the members of the Tucson raiding party were all acquitted. Cargill was burned in effigy for his part in supporting Lieutenant Whitman's efforts, and it was the end of Whitman's military career.

However, the episode did not escape the attention of Washington, and President Grant, who described the attack as 'purely murder', was insistent that action should be taken to bring stability to the area. Two months after the Camp Grant massacre, General Crook was in Tucson. His role was to bring the Apache into reservations and keep them there, and initially he was successful. By the time he left Arizona to go north, in 1875, several of the Apache leaders had succumbed, including Chief Cochise of the Chiricahuas. The challenge was to keep them in reservations usually located at a distance from familiar territory, in conditions that were often meagre and demeaning. Crook would have to return to finish the job, but in the meantime he was needed in Wyoming and Montana.

Forty years earlier, Washington Irving had made his 'tour on the prairies' and responded excitedly when he met members of the Osage tribe. He celebrated 'the glorious independence of man in a savage state', and was particularly struck by a young warrior 'with his rifle, his blanket, and his horse... ready at a moment's warning to rove the world; he carried all his worldly effects with him, and in the absence of artificial wants, possessed the great secret of personal freedom'. With something like envy, Irving highlighted a comparison with those who were slaves to society: 'our superfluities are the chains that bind us, impeding every movement of our bodies and thwarting every impulse of our souls'.

When in the 1850s Laurence Oliphant travelled in Minnesota, in what was then still described as 'the far west', he was much impressed by his encounters with the Chippewa. He described a Chippewa chief:

> ... standing proudly erect under his plume of hawk's feathers, that betokened a warrior who had taken in his day many a Sioux scalp. His red blanket, worked with many devices, was thrown gracefully over his shoulder; his belt was garnished with tomahawk and scalping knife, and in his hand he held a handsomely mounted rifle. His feet were encased in richly embroidered moccasins, with fringed leggings reaching to his thigh. Altogether, his costume exhibited a combination of ribbons, feathers, beads, and paint, which was wonderfully becoming.

By this time, however dramatic the spectacle, it was no longer possible to be carried away by romantic notions of independence. Oliphant condemned the policy of 'deportation', which he predicted would 'retard their civilisation' and eventually 'exterminate these original possessors of the soil'. In his view, the solution was to incorporate the natives into 'industrious and energetic' communities of 'Anglo-Saxons', which he believed would encourage them to adopt 'the arts of peace'. As things were, they were landed with the worst of both worlds:

> As soon as the existence of an Indian population is found to interfere with white settlement, they are moved just far enough west to be beyond the influence of a really civilised community, but not far enough to escape the contaminating effects of contact with those unscrupulous adventurers, who hover like hawks upon the outskirts of civilisation.

By the 1870s it was probably too late for a change in policy, even if the political will had existed.

On 29 May 1876, General Crook rode out of Fort Fetterman on the North Platte River with over a thousand men, heading north. An ultimatum had been issued to the Sioux and Cheyenne, requiring them all to come into the reservations. One chief who had been identified as particularly problematic was Crazy Horse of the Oglala Sioux, who John Bourke rated as 'one of the great soldiers of his day and generation'. Crazy Horse had, in Bourke's view, 'a great admiration for Crook, which was reciprocated'. Crook and his men camped on the banks of the Rosebud, not far from a very large encampment of Sioux. The Sioux attacked. The following day General Crook was in retreat. It was the opening round in a campaign that involved the crushing defeat of General George Armstrong Custer's 7th Cavalry at the Little Big Horn, and the eventual surrender of the Sioux and Cheyenne. Armstrong is, of course, a name from the Scottish Borders and Custer is an Orkney name.

Crook's force was part of a three-pronged invasion, with Colonel Gibbon in Montana and Brigadier General Terry in South Dakota, whose troops included the 7th Cavalry. It was Custer's rash bid for glory that resulted in him leading 224 men to annihilation by a combined force of Sioux and Cheyenne: a disaster for the US government, and ultimately a disaster for the Indians, as they were rounded up with renewed determination and herded into reservations. But it wasn't a quick or easy process. Generals Crook and Terry hunted the Sioux in Montana and South Dakota with exhausted troops and little success. It was several months before they were in a position to mount a sustained campaign, with Crazy Horse as their main target.

In November, 11 companies of infantry, 11 of cavalry and four of artillery, plus Indian scouts, 168 wagons, seven ambulances and 400 pack mules again set off from Fort Fetterman. It is no surprise to find Scottish names among the troops: Major G.A. Gordon, Captain J.B. Campbell, James Allison, John Hamilton, another Campbell, an Anderson, and others. The troops penetrated the Big Horn Mountains, where they found a Cheyenne village. Crook sent cavalry under Colonel Ranald Mackenzie to capture it; they attacked and destroyed the village, killing more than 40 warriors. Those who escaped joined Crazy Horse, who was eventually persuaded to accept reservation life. Crook promised that his people would not be removed from buffalo country. When the Sioux surrendered, there was an eruption of rejoicing in Deadwood. There was, in the words of John Bourke, 'much in the way of bonfires, the firing of salutes from anvils, cheerings, mass-meetings, alleged music, and no small portion of hard drinking'. Crook was given the freedom of Deadwood, such as it was.

Bands of Cheyenne surrendered at Fort Robinson, assuming that they would be assigned to reservations alongside their allies, the Sioux. Instead, they were sent south to Indian Territory, but with a promise from Crook that if it did not suit them, they could return. When they arrived at Fort Reno they were met by Colonel Mackenzie, who took from them their horses and their few remaining weapons. They were expected to settle into a life of farming. But Indian Territory was notoriously barren and rations were sparse. The Cheyenne, already weak, had few resources against famine and sickness, and many died. Mackenzie was indignant on their behalf: 'I am expected to see that Indians behave properly whom the government is starving – and not only that, but starving in flagrant violation of agreement.' Eventually the Cheyenne were allowed to take back their horses so they could hunt buffalo, but there were no buffalo. The once vast herds had been destroyed by white hunters for their skins and to feed railroad workers.

The consequent break-out of the Cheyenne, desperate to return to their own country and to keep themselves alive, has been chronicled in *Cheyenne Autumn* (1953), the book by Mari Sandoz which was the basis of John Ford's film of the same name (1964). The episode is also the subject of Howard Fast's compelling novel *The Last Frontier* (1966). Generals Crook and Mackenzie were key players. In September 1878 about 280 Cheyenne, two-thirds of them women and children, quietly slipped away from the Indian Territory reservation and headed north, led by chiefs Dull Knife and Little Wolf. On the way they stole horses to speed their progress, and cattle to provide food. Wild rumours circulated of Cheyenne attacks and depredations. They were, according to Edgar Bronson whose Nebraska ranch was not far from the route they took, 'ravaging the country, and killing all who came in their path'. Such accounts proved to be much exaggerated. The Cheyenne in fact were trying to stay under cover and attract as little attention as possible.

The Cheyenne had mixed feelings about Crook and Mackenzie. It was Dull Knife's village that Mackenzie had attacked in the aftermath of Little Big Horn, and his son had been killed. Little Wolf was with Dull Knife, and was badly wounded. But they acknowledged that both Crook and Mackenzie had a genuine concern for the Cheyenne. As Mari Sandoz put it, 'Mackenzie seemed a good man, doing what he must, as was the one over him [Crook]'. US troops, 10,000 in all, were quickly on the trail of the Cheyenne and civilians joined in the chase. At first their quarry was elusive – there were demands that Crook be court-martialled because of his failure to recapture what was described as a marauding horde. His evident sympathy did not play well with those convinced that they were dealing with uncontrollable savages. 'I do not wonder,' Crook commented, 'and you will not either that when these Indians see their wives and children starving and their last source of supplies cut off, they go to war. And then we are sent out to kill them.' The American public was not in a mood to respond positively. The Cheyenne recognised that Crook was trying to act on their behalf. 'He was a good man,' said Wooden Leg, 'always kind to the Indians.'

Inevitably, the Cheyenne were tracked down, and the remnant that survived attack, the winter cold and hunger, was settled on a reservation on the Yellowstone. Crook was convinced that they should be allowed to remain in the north. In his report on the Cheyenne outbreak, he reminded the authorities that:

> Among these Cheyenne Indians were some of the bravest and most efficient of the auxiliaries who had acted under General Mackenzie

and myself in the campaign against the hostile Sioux in 1876 and
1877, and I still preserve grateful remembrance of their distinguished services, which the government seems to have forgotten.

The efforts to secure the frontier would have cost a great deal more
in time, money and lives if there had not been Native Americans
prepared to support these efforts: Crook was one of the few to
acknowledge that. Dull Knife and Little Wolf lived into old age,
but not surprisingly they felt bitter and isolated. With General Crook
both pursuing and supporting them, they had in a sense won. They
were not sent back to Indian Territory. But more than half of those
who six months before had started the trek north, never made it.

Crook's frontier tasks were not complete. The Apache were
growing increasingly restive, and in 1883 bands under Geronimo and
Chato broke out of their reservations. Crook pursued them, with the
help of Apache scouts commanded by Captain Emmet Crawford,
another of Scots descent and veteran of the Sioux campaign, and
Archie McIntosh, part-Scottish, part-Chippewa, and Crook's most
valued scout. McIntosh, born in Michigan, was the son of a Hudson's
Bay Company trader. At the age of 12 he was sent to relatives in
Edinburgh for two years of education. In 1855, after spending a
year working for the Bay Company as a clerk, he became a US
Army scout, at first in the Columbia River area. With Donald
McKay, also of mixed Indian and Scottish origins, he rescued a
troop of US soldiers from annihilation. Another exploit that helped
cement his reputation occurred in Oregon in the winter of 1867,
when he led General Crook to safety through a blizzard.

In the 1870s McIntosh was with Crook in the south, hunting
hostile Apache. On Christmas Day 1872 he guided an attack led by
Lieutenant William Ross on Apache camped by the Salt River in
Arizona. The Apache were taken by surprise, and 66 of them were
killed. By the early 1880s the situation on the Apache reservations
was deteriorating. Although there were some Indian agents who
put huge efforts into making the reservations viable and helping

their charges to adapt, there were many others who exploited them, or colluded in their exploitation. Supplies intended for the reservations were sold on, while no effort was made to prevent white settlers intruding on land designated as Apache. In fact, there were those who deliberately tried to provoke Indians to violence, so that reservation land could be taken over.

In September 1881, Geronimo and other Apache chiefs, with about 70 men, slipped away from the White Mountain reservation in Arizona and headed south towards the Mexican border. Six months later they returned and persuaded many more to join them in a bid to recover their old life in Mexico. The man charged with their pursuit was Scottish-American Colonel George Forsyth, who caught up with them at Horse Shoe Canyon, near the border. The Apache managed to fight off the US troops while the main contingent crossed into Mexico, only to encounter a Mexican infantry regiment which immediately attacked, killing large numbers of women and children. Among those who escaped were Geronimo and Chato.

The reservations were in chaos, the remaining inmates increasingly embittered and disaffected, while the possibility threatened of raids from breakaway Apache. General Crook was called back to take command of the Department of Arizona. His first step was to meet with Apache on the White Mountain reservation and listen to their grievances. If earlier in his career he had taken a hard line against the Apache, he had learnt that they deserved to be treated with respect. There were few officials who shared that view. The Apache were prevented from supporting themselves in the old ways, and deprived of other means of survival. They had been systematically cheated and lied to for so long they no longer had faith in government promises. Crook gave specific instructions to his men as to their dealings with the Apache, his pragmatism reflected in an order issued by him in October 1882:

> In all their dealings with the Indians, officers must be careful not only to observe the strictest fidelity, but to make no promises not

in their power to carry out; all grievances arising within their jurisdiction should be redressed, so that an accumulation of them may not cause an outbreak.

It did not take Crook long to grasp the nature of these grievances: 'I discovered immediately that a general feeling of mistrust of our people existed among all the bands of Apaches.' They did not talk readily, but when he finally got through the barrier of suspicion his conclusion was that they had 'not only the best reasons for complaining, but had displayed remarkable forbearance in remaining at peace'. Crook was determined to make changes: 'we are too culpable, as a nation, for the existing condition of affairs. It follows that we must satisfy them that hereafter they shall be treated with justice, and protected from inroads of white men.'

The Apache were given more freedom as to where they could locate their homes within the reservation, and white squatters were forced to leave. Rations were no longer diverted to line the pockets of unscrupulous agents. The Apache were allowed a degree of self-government, organising their own policing and holding their own courts. Meanwhile, Geronimo and the others were still in Mexico, and inevitably a trickle of warriors left White Mountain to join them. Crook knew that until they were brought in the chapter could not be closed. There would always be a threat of raids, and a continuing destabilisation of reservation life.

Crook prepared a force to bring in Geronimo. Agreement with the Mexican government meant that he could not cross into Mexico unless there were Apache raids into the US. In March 1883 Apache raided a mining camp near Tombstone, which gave Crook the excuse he needed, and he entered Mexico. He captured Geronimo's village while the chief and his warriors were stealing cattle from Mexican ranchers and clashing with Mexican troops. With Crook was Archie McIntosh. Geronimo agreed to bring his people back to San Carlos on the White Mountain reservation. Nearly 400 Apache men, women and children returned with Crook. Geronimo and Chato, however, remained in Mexico. Geronimo had proposed that they would stay to gather together scattered members of the tribe, and bring them in later. Eight months later, that was exactly what they did.

It still wasn't the end. In May 1885, Geronimo was off again, with 34 men and 100 women and children. He was convinced the authorities were going to arrest and possibly hang him. Again he made for Mexico, and again Crook crossed the border in pursuit, still determined to talk rather than attack. Again, Geronimo was persuaded to return, with Crook promising that although it was probable that Geronimo and his people would be sent to confinement on a reservation in Florida, after two years they would be allowed back to Arizona. But on the way north Geronimo broke away again. Crook was reprimanded by the US War Department for making such a promise, and for what was identified as negligence. He was regarded as being altogether too sympathetic towards the Indians. Command was handed over to General Nelson Miles, and it was his officers who were responsible for Geronimo's final surrender. He was sent to Florida, along with many other Apache, including scouts who had assisted the army. They had a miserable time in the Florida swamps, so utterly different from the mountains and deserts of their own country. Many of them died.

There were a few whites who didn't forget them, among them George Crook and Lieutenant Hugh Scott. Arizona was determined to keep the Apache out, but through Lieutenant Scott the Kiowa and Comanche offered them a home on their reservation at Fort Sill, Texas. There they settled in 1894, and there Geronimo died in 1909. Archie McIntosh married a woman from San Carlos, and settled on the reservation, where he and his descendants were prominent in local affairs. Captain Crawford, latterly based at San Carlos, was killed by Mexican irregulars in 1886, when he crossed the border and attacked a Chiricahua camp in Sonora. George Crook spent his last years at Omaha, as Commanding General of the Department of the Platte. He died in Chicago in 1890. The physician who attended him was called McClellan.

In dozens of Westerns the Apache are portrayed as a particularly savage and often sinister foe. Among the soldiers and scouts who confront them are many Scottish names. In John Prebble's story 'My Great-Aunt Appearing-Day' (in *Spanish Stirrup and Other Stories*, 1958), Lieutenant Fraser is an inexperienced 'West Pointer', an admirer of General Custer, and has an over-enthusiastic contempt for Indians. (The Frasers had a long history of military activity in North America: the Fraser Highlanders fought in the French and Indian War of 1755–63.) But in Louis L'Amour's *Hondo* (1953), filmed in 1954 with John Wayne as the eponymous hero and in 1967 with Robert Taylor, Lieutenant McKay leads his troop of cavalry in pursuit of a band of marauding Apache. McKay is young and untested; dismounted, he walks straight backed 'as if on a drill field', but, in Hondo's view, he passes muster: 'Young, but he would grow into it. Proud, the way a young man should be, but conscious there was much to learn.' As the column moves off 'the dust rose around them, then settled slowly, and the sun shone brightly on the last of the horses, glinting from the carbines'. As the riders disappear, Hondo reflects: 'Somewhere out there on some sun-blasted slope the Apaches would be waiting. Somewhere out there men would die.' The cavalry do battle with the Indians and McKay returns wounded but undefeated. The battered and bloody troops ride into the parade ground, while 'westward the land was bright with the setting sun'. The Scottish soldier is well and truly written into frontier legend.

One after another the tribes in the western states and territories were pressured into reservations. The route west to Oregon and California had become a highway. Santa Fe and the southwest beckoned. The northwest was attracting settlement. Discoveries of gold and silver meant that people were flooding into areas that previously had attracted little interest. The vast herds of buffalo, staple of the Plains tribes, were disappearing. The railroads were carving up traditional hunting grounds. Those Native Americans who resisted these pressures struck out with increasing intensity.

For some, the only way to deal with Indians was with 'powder, not prayer', in the words of Scottish American Charles Ferguson, whose views on Native Americans were very different from Laurence Oliphant's: 'I never knew but one "truly good" Indian, and he was dead... All I have ever known have been cowardly and treacherous, never attack like men, but crawl upon you, three or four to one, and shoot you down.' The Indian 'is the emigrant's enemy' and the emigrant should attack, rather than wait to be attacked. But there were others from Scotland who shared Oliphant's more sympathetic perspective on the 'Indian problem'. In 1873, Isabella Bird, born in Yorkshire but a resident of Scotland when she was not travelling, was in Colorado. In her view:

> The Americans will never solve the Indian problem till the Indian is extinct. They have treated them after a fashion which has intensified their treachery and 'devilry' as enemies, and as friends reduces them to a degraded pauperism, devoid of the very first elements of civilisation... The Indian Agency has been a sink of fraud and corruption; it is said that only 30 per cent of the allowance ever reaches those for whom it is voted.

Six years later Robert Louis Stevenson observed the consequences of this treatment in Native American families 'disgracefully dressed out with the sweepings of civilisation', and echoes Bird's remarks. He commented on 'the silent stoicism of their conduct, and the pathetic degradation of their appearance' and the jeering behaviour towards them of his fellow-passengers, which made him 'ashamed for the thing we call civilisation,' adding, 'We should carry upon our consciences so much at least, of our forefathers' misconduct as we continue to profit by ourselves.'

In 1875, President Grant confirmed that the Wallowa Valley in Oregon was to be 'withheld from entry and settlement as public lands, and that the same be set apart as a reservation for the roaming Nez Perce, as recommended by the Secretary of Interior and the Commissioner for Indian Affairs'. Two years later the valley was made available for settlement, and the Nez Perce were instructed to leave and go to another reservation. Their leader, Chief Joseph, believed there was no choice but to comply, although the deadline imposed gave them no time to gather their stock. But some of the chiefs were determined to resist and Joseph felt he had to support them. The Nez Perce defeated US troops at White Bird Canyon, and then fled north. Their only refuge now was across the border in Canada.

There followed months of flight, fighting and pursuit. All that summer and into the autumn Joseph led his people over mountain peaks and through narrow passes with the army at his heels. When they camped by the Big Hole River, hoping for some respite to hunt for game, they were attacked by Colonel John Gibbon. With him were at least three Scots-born soldiers, one of whom, Private Malcolm MacGregor, deserted. Many women and children were killed, but they didn't give up, continuing their trek and fighting rearguard actions. Winter overtook them, and cold and hunger were factors in Chief Joseph's eventual, and inevitable, decision to surrender. 'The little children are freezing to death,' he said. And went on to utter words that are among the best remembered and resonant Native American statements: 'My heart is sick and sad. From where the sun now stands I will fight no more for ever.'

The Nez Perce were sent, like the Cheyenne, to a reservation in Indian Territory, and like the Cheyenne they were miserably unhappy there. But a few evaded capture and with Chief White Bird crossed into Canada, where they joined the camp of Sitting Bull who had fled there after the Little Big Horn. A relative of White Bird was a man called Duncan MacDonald, the son of fur trader Angus MacDonald and his Nez Perce wife Catherine, who had been ranching in Montana since 1846. Duncan was born at Fort Connah, north of Missoula, and grew up at Fort Colvile near the Canadian border.

Duncan MacDonald followed White Bird to Canada, where he interviewed him and other Nez Perce, which enabled him to put together a detailed account of the Nez Perce experience. The result was a series of articles published in the *New North West* newspaper in 1879, written from the Indian perspective. He described the sleeping camp at Big Hole, the surprise attack by Gibbon's soldiers, the 'shameful' slaughter of women and children. And, aware of his own Scottish Highland origins, he likened Indian tribes to the clans. This almost certainly explained his ability to use his trans-cultural position to mediate between white and Indian, and he became a spokesman for and to the Nez Perce people. 'From my mother and from my long association with the Indians, I have learned to have a thorough understanding of Indian things. Today I think of and view things about me with Indian eyes.' He might have added that he had inherited from his Scottish background an acute eye for exploitation. 'The strong oppresses the weak,' he wrote, 'and power is always power, right or wrong.' Descendants of Angus and Duncan MacDonald still live in Montana.

By the 1880s there was a growing sense that the frontier was closing. For potential settlers this engendered anxiety that land was running out, and there was pressure to open Indian Territory for settlement. It duly happened in 1889. For the Native Americans it meant they were victims of a cynical disregard for the 1887 Dawes Act which had granted them the right to own land on the same basis as whites. The pattern of depriving Natives of land provided for them as part of the solution to the 'Indian problem' was being repeated.

Fort Robinson in Nebraska was located within a large but shrinking area designated as a reservation for the Sioux. The pressures of settlement and the scramble for gold and other minerals ate away at reservation land, and individuals who drew attention to the plight of tribes struggling to survive with minimal support were not dealt with kindly. Many people resented the fact that money was being spent on people who, in their eyes, did little to help themselves. And there was still plenty of opportunity to siphon off provisions and supplies that should have reached the reservation.

The leading Sioux chiefs were dead or growing old. Crazy Horse, so much respected by General Crook, was by 1877 living on the reservation, but in September of that year, he was arrested; word had reached Crook that he was planning to break out. He was brought to Fort Robinson, where in a scuffle he was bayoneted, and died later that night. In 1881, Sitting Bull and 186 of his followers returned to the US from Canada. At Fort Buford in North Dakota, he surrendered. Although a promise had been made that he could live on the Standing Rock reservation, he was kept as a prisoner at Fort Randall, further south on the Missouri. Over a year later he was finally allowed to go to Standing Rock, where the agent was a man called James McLaughlin. It was his task to complete the taming of the Sioux.

General Crook's association with the Sioux was not over. The government in Washington wished to release more reservation land for settlement, and in 1888 sent a commission to investigate. When the commissioners failed to persuade Sitting Bull and the Sioux to part with land for 50 cents an acre, Crook was called in and authorised to offer $1.50 an acre. They knew he was well regarded by the Indians, and hoped that he would get them to agree. Some chiefs signed, but Sitting Bull and a few others held out. McLaughlin organised a final meeting to get the signatures of all remaining chiefs, but deliberately did not inform Sitting Bull. He arrived anyway, but it was too late. The reservation was broken up into smaller areas, with the surrounding land now open to white settlement. Sitting Bull's disgust at the capitulation of his comrades was expressed in his comment: 'There are no Indians left but me!'

This was the context for what is often portrayed as the final chapter of Indian resistance, although it is perhaps more accurately described as a late and tragic example of white panic, if not cynical opportunism. It was a Scottish American who was in command of the troops involved in the episode. It was triggered by the spread of the Ghost Dance cult, which had attracted a large following from Indians desperate to believe that their traditional way of life would be recovered. The cult arrived at Standing Rock in the autumn of 1890, and was described by McLaughlin as 'pernicious'. Alarmed at what was interpreted as the possibility of insurrection, the army moved in, although there were those who advised restraint.

Events moved rapidly. On 15 December Sitting Bull was shot while 'resisting arrest' and turmoil ensued. Distressed and confused, Sitting Bull's people began to make their way to Pine Ridge where they hoped they would be safe. They were intercepted by soldiers of the 7th Cavalry, the regiment once commanded by General Custer now under the command of Colonel James Forsyth. The band of 350 Sioux, 230 of them women and children, were escorted to Wounded Knee Creek, where they were issued with basic provisions and told to camp. They were guarded by a ring of troopers and two rapid-firing Hotchkiss guns. The Sioux chief, Big Foot, was gravely ill with pneumonia.

The next morning Colonel Forsyth called for the Sioux to give up their weapons, searching their tents and their persons to ensure that nothing was overlooked. When almost at the end of the process a gun went off, possibly fired by a young man called Black Coyote who had protested at being parted from his Winchester. Instantly the soldiers began to fire indiscriminately into the assembled Sioux. Some fought back with what weapons remained; others tried to escape. Around 300 were killed. It was 29 December and bitterly cold. The wounded were taken in wagons to Pine Ridge; the dead were left, to be covered by falling snow.

The massacre at Wounded Knee Creek, usually seen as the closing episode of the Indian wars, has become an emblem of white cruelty and government hypocrisy. But an official investigation came to the conclusion that the Sioux had behaved treacherously, that most of those killed had fallen to Indian bullets, that in the circumstances the killing of women and children was inevitable, and that 'the Indians at Wounded Knee brought about their own destruction as surely as any people ever did'.

With the Scottish reputation for soldiering, it is not surprising that Scottish names appear frequently in accounts of the Indian wars. It can safely be assumed that there were many more who do not appear in the record, ordinary troopers as well as officers. Among them would be many of Highland descent who may have recognised, as Duncan MacDonald did, analogies between the displacement of America's native population and that of Highlanders from their homeland. There are striking examples of Scottish Americans who were sympathetic to the plight of the Native Americans, including some who were part Indian themselves, but there was little they could do to resist the pressures of population. As Crook said to the Sioux in 1889: '[the white men] are still coming, and will come until they overrun all of this country; and you can't prevent it'.

CHAPTER 4

Overlanders and Homesteaders

... westward we rolled
Your desert was hot and your mountains were cold.

'Pastures of Plenty', Woody Guthrie

FIVE YEARS AFTER the Oregon Treaty of 1846 settled the future of the territory south of the 49th parallel, ensuring that the future states of Oregon and Washington would become part of the US, the legislature of Oregon Territory sent a memorial to Congress. It needed a safe and practical route to bring people and supplies across the plains and the mountains. And it needed the right kind of people, 'the hardy pioneer of the western states, for upon him, and those of like habits of industry and vigor, depends the force necessary to prostrate these mighty forests, and lay bare the hidden treasures of [Oregon's] prolific timbered soil'.

The Scottish-born newspaper editor James Gordon Bennett, who had left Keith in Banffshire in 1819, was strongly in favour of the US acquisition of Oregon and Washington, and in the New York *Herald* presented a heroic picture of overland travellers, calling for Congress to support the 'hardy Western pioneers'. Back in Scotland there was continuing interest in the American frontier, but it was predicted by the *Edinburgh Review* that Oregon would 'never be colonised from the Eastern states'.

There was no doubt that to create the overland route demanded by Oregon would require commitment, effort and extraordinary stamina. Supply posts were needed, and the army to provide protection. But in the early 1840s, when the first wagon trains began to lumber across the prairies, the pioneers were on their own, with only guides and a few scattered trading posts to help them on their way. It has been estimated that between 1840 and 1848 about 11,500 people made their way to Oregon, and slightly less than 3,000 to California. With the discovery of gold in the Sacramento Valley numbers would change dramatically, with nearly 200,000 going overland to California in the next 12 years. On one day in May 1850, a thousand wagons passed Fort Kearney on the River Platte. That same year saw nearly 10 times that number pass Fort Laramie, further west, on a single day in August, with around 39,500 men. Two years later wagons 12 abreast were leaving St Joseph, one of the departure points on the Missouri. None of the attempts to portray this extraordinary migration in fiction or film has quite captured its immensity.

In 1842, a wagon train set off from Elm Grove, Missouri, near Independence, organised by Elijah White, who had been offered the post of Indian agent in Oregon. His party of over a hundred people and 18 wagons included the two part-Chinook sons of Thomas McKay, formerly of the Astoria Fur Company, who had helped a much earlier expedition to Oregon led by Jason Lee. Lee's intention was to found a Methodist mission in the territory. That same year, 1834, McKay built Fort Boise where the Boise River meets the Snake. He also assisted the more famous Marcus Whitman and Henry Spalding expedition two years later. The two McKay boys, John and Alexander, were returning to Oregon after a spell at school in the east. Other Scottish names in the White party were Hugh Burns, blacksmith, and Medorem Crawford from New York, who kept a journal of the trip.

Historian of the West David Lavender describes White's expedition as a 'prototype', and lists the features which would be replicated in many later journeys. White hired a mountain man as guide, an essential first step. Two members of the party were killed in separate incidents when guns went off accidentally, another drowned in the Snake River. Two couples were married on the trail. There were discipline problems and power struggles – White's leadership was challenged, and eventually he was ousted. As a consequence, he and a few followers left the main group, only to rejoin them at Fort Laramie, for reasons of security. Misadventures, marriages and quarrels played a part in most subsequent overland journeys.

The White wagon train continued on its way, still following the North Platte until it reached the Sweetwater and made a sharp turn south. The emigrants followed the Sweetwater, then sheered off through South Pass shadowed but not attacked by Sioux. At Green River, White again parted from the main group, believing that the wagons should be abandoned and packhorses used instead. At Fort Hall, Richard Grant advised that wheels would not negotiate the next stage to Fort Walla Walla, so the eight remaining wagons were exchanged for horses and supplies. They pressed on, with Medorem Crawford and others in the rear, urging on the weary cattle. They were following the Snake River. Crawford commented on the 'frightful precipices of Burnt Canyon... In many places if our animals had made one mis-step it would be certain death.' Then came 'sandy country' where they 'suffered considerable for water as the day was exceedingly hot'. In the evening they reached a creek: 'never was water to me more acceptable though of a very indifferent quality'. A little further on they found 'boiling water running out of the ground'.

Ahead rose the Blue Mountains which 'struck us with terror'. They had to be crossed to reach the mission near Fort Walla Walla which was run by Marcus Whitman. The cattle were exhausted, and moved so slowly that they got to the mission several days after White and his party. 'I was never more pleased to see a house or white people in my life,' wrote Crawford. After a few days rest and recuperation, Crawford and those with him set off again, following the Columbia River downstream until the narrow gorge made progress impossible and they had to head once again into the mountains where they followed an old Indian trail that precariously negotiated a rocky terrain sliced by chasms and torrential watercourses. At last they reached the Willamette, where beside the falls John McLoughlin of

Fort Vancouver would soon found Oregon City. It became home for many of those who had been on the trail for four months. Crawford himself in 1847 became a member of Oregon's provisional legislature and then of the state legislature. In the early 1860s he helped to lead more wagon trains into Oregon, before taking up civic roles, first as Oregon's collector of internal revenue and then as appraiser of customs. He made the transition, as many did, from pioneer to solid citizen.

John McLoughlin, his associate Inverness doctor William Tolmie, and Hudson's Bay Company fur-trader John McLeod were all noted for the help they gave to early settlers. Like Thomas McKay, McLeod helped the Spalding and Whitman Presbyterian missionary families on their journey through the Rockies. The mission the Whitmans established near present-day Walla Walla in Washington spearheaded settlement but ended in tragedy 11 years later when members of the Cayuse tribe, provoked by the belief that white settlers had brought with them measles that killed hundreds of their people, murdered Marcus and Narcissa Whitman and several other whites.

Two years after the White expedition, the grandson of a Scottish Borders family set off on the Oregon Trail at the age of 22. John Minto was a coal miner from Pittsburgh, and although what immediately propelled him was a miners' strike, he had always had a hankering to go west. 'If I live,' he said, 'I will go across the Rocky Mountains.' He travelled with a family called Morrison (probably also of Scottish origins) who virtually adopted him. In exchange for bed and board he provided labour. He was active and courageous, and a keen buffalo hunter. Like every wagon train, they made a pause at Fort Laramie, to rest, catch up with the laundry and replenish supplies. Minto has left an evocative description:

> We had a beautiful camp on the bank of the Laramie, and both weather and scene were delightful. The moon, I think, must have been near the full... at all events we levelled off a space and one man played the fiddle and we danced into the night.

He visited a Sioux camp, smoked a peace pipe with Sioux warriors, and attracted the attention of Sioux girls who attempted to purchase him from Mrs Morrison.

West of Fort Laramie the country was, in Minto's words, 'a rich game park, and swarming with all animals that prey upon game, the large wolf and grizzly bear being most seen'. Although it was August, and there were now worries that they would not make it through the mountains before snow came, the men diverted themselves with hunting buffalo, killing more than could be used for meat. But typhoid fever hit the travellers. One of the first to die was a young girl, and Minto, much distressed, helped to dig her grave by the Sweetwater: 'From my eight years in the coal mines, I had seen men and boys maimed, crushed or buried by machinery, falling roofs or firedamp, but nothing of that kind affected like this death scene.' Two weeks later he was burying a second typhoid victim.

They traversed South Pass and bore south to Fort Bridger, then northwest to Fort Hall on the Snake River. Minto, impatient perhaps at the slow progress of the wagons, decided to press on ahead on horseback with a young man called Daniel Clark. But one night his horse bolted, scared off by wolves, and Minto was left without a mount until a Shoshone lent him a horse. When Minto and Clark at last arrived at Fort Hall, they were penniless and hungry. Minto had only his gun to offer in exchange for another horse, but eventually persuaded Richard Grant to effect the transaction. Undeterred by his experiences, Minto did not rejoin the wagons when they left Fort Hall, but set off with two others a few days later. One by one, they overtook most of the wagon trains on the trail in front of them, and with the help of Indian guides made good progress through the Blue Mountains and on to the Columbia. It was now October. They followed the river down to the Dalles where they left it to cross the Cascades to the Willamette. They arrived at Oregon City on 18 October.

The whole trip was beset by quarrels and factions, as Elijah White's expedition had been. Perhaps it was inevitable. The wagon trains were composed of people of mixed resources and experience, and with differing views of how things should be managed. There were families with young children, and single male adventurers – single women unattached to families were rare. There were some who had to scrape together the funds for a wagon, beasts and essential supplies, and others who had to abandon much of what they took as they were overloaded. Most had little idea of what the journey entailed and many were ill-equipped to deal with exhaustion, hunger, thirst, Indian attacks, frustration, sickness, gruesome accidents and the loss of family members.

In 1845 a huge wagon train, split into sections, left Independence. At Fort Hall a contingent peeled off for California, but most of the emigrants were making for Oregon. When they reached the fearsome Columbia River and found no boats for the final stretch of their journey, there were different opinions about the best route to take. One group, under Stephen Meek (a Scottish name), took what was believed to be a short cut to the southern Willamette Valley, and got into desperate difficulties. The emigrants were so furious with their guide that they threatened to kill him. Another group followed Joel Palmer and Samuel Barlow, a Scot whose intention was to help build a wagon road through the Cascades, on another overland route which took them south of Mt Hood. To get their wagons through they had to hack and burn huge trees, but it was October by this time and they were overtaken by snow. They struggled on, until a rescue party arrived from Oregon City. Among the rescuers were Peter Stewart and Matthew and Charles Gilmore.

Although there were often quarrels and disagreements among the emigrants, and sometimes outbreaks of violence, without collaboration and mutual support many would not have made it to their destination. Another party that had to be rescued were the 1,500 led by Elijah Elliott. They attempted the Malheur River route, branching off from the Snake way to the south of the more usual routes, lost their way and ran out of food. John Ross commanded a band of militiamen based in Jacksonville, who patrolled the west end of the southern route and came to their aid.

Not everyone travelled by wagon or on horseback. A Scottish American called Brookmire, from Pennsylvania, was one of four men who in 1850 pushed wheelbarrows to California. The Mormons, who in July 1847 had entered Salt Lake Valley and founded their City of Zion, organised extraordinary overland journeys with hand-carts. From 1839, the Mormons actively recruited in Scotland, with considerable success. One Mormon Elder in Edinburgh commented: 'The people of Scotland are slow to believe and embrace the truth, but after they have embraced it, they are firm, yea, they would lay down their lives for the truth.' Several thousand Scots crossed the Atlantic to join the Mormon emigration west. There was a system in place to get them there, and they were looked after and guided along the way. David Lavender describes those who gathered in Iowa City in the summer of 1856, 'more women than men, more children under 15 than either'. Many were elderly, and most showed all the signs of years if not decades of deprivation: 'starved cheeks, pale skins, bad teeth, thin chests'.

They had sailed from Liverpool, inspired by the message of the Mormon missionaries: 'the gathering poor, if they are faithful, have a right to feel that the favor of God, angels, and holy men is enlisted in their behalf'. But along with the exhortations to salvation came warnings:

> None of the emigrating Saints have ever crossed the plains who have had greater demands on the shepherds of their flock, than those who will travel in the handcart companies the coming season... It is our constant desire not to mislead the Saints concerning the difficulties of the journey to Utah. We wish them calmly to make up their minds that it is not an easy task, and to start with faith, trusting in Israel's God.

Among the missionaries and organisers Scottish names appear, George Grant, for example, and Daniel McArthur. Alexander Wright and Samuel Mulliner were early Scottish converts who conducted the first mission to Scotland, appealing particularly in Glasgow, Edinburgh and Aberdeen, and the industrial Lowlands.

In June 1856 the emigrants set off from Iowa City, pulling handcarts loaded with between 400 and 500 pounds of goods and supplies. They travelled in three companies, one led by Daniel McArthur. Some were already sick. There had been deaths and there would be more on the road. More than three months and 1,300 miles later they emerged out of Emigration Canyon into Salt Lake Valley to be greeted by Brigham Young and a brass band. One hand-cart puller was David Adamson from Dunfermline. Later Scottish arrivals were the Campbell family, from Bo'ness in West Lothian. Thomas Campbell had been a collier, moving around Fife, Lanarkshire and the Lothians with his wife Elisabeth and their growing, but later diminishing, family. Eight of their 13 children died of smallpox. They joined the Church of the Latter Day Saints in 1848, and in 1866 left for America. By 1868 they were farming in Utah, and later Thomas was in Salt Lake City working in the quarry that provided stone for the city's great Temple. (Many other Scots would work at quarrying in Utah.) Thomas Campbell was badly injured by falling rock, and never recovered.

It is impossible to know how many Scottish Americans took the overland trail to Oregon and California, but Scottish names regularly appear in the various accounts. Peter Burnett and his family – Burnett is a Border and an Aberdeenshire name – left Missouri, where he had a store and heavy debts, to join the large migration of 1843. It had been instigated by the Applegate brothers, Jesse, Charles and – another Scottish name – Lindsay. Many years later Jesse Applegate wrote of the gathering emigrants that they had 'no previous preparation, relying only on the fertility of their invention'. They faced a journey of 2,000 miles:

> The way lies over trackless wastes, wide and deep rivers, rugged and lofty mountains, and is beset with hostile savages. Yet, whether

it were a deep river with no tree upon its bank, a rugged defile where even a loose horse could not pass, a hill too steep for him to climb, or a threatened attack of an enemy, they are always found ready and equal to the occasion, and always conquerors. May we not call them men of destiny?

The Burnett family loaded their possessions into two wagons with teams of oxen and themselves into a lighter horse-drawn wagon, and in May, rendezvoused at Elm Grove, north of Independence, with over a thousand others. It was a congenial gathering, full of chat and 'the sound of joyous music'. 'Our long journey,' Peter Burnett recounted decades later in his *Recollections and Opinions of an Old Pioneer* (1880), 'thus began in sunshine and song, in anecdote and laughter; but these all vanished before we reached its termination.' Also assembled was a family called Stewart, whose daughter was born en route to Oregon.

The large wagon train left the Missouri towards the end of May, rather late in the season. Burnett was voted captain. They were soon encountering challenging river crossings and prairie storms. There were divisions between those with a large quantity of livestock and those without. Jesse Applegate took charge of the former. A month of travelling took them to the Platte River, and by the end of July they had reached the foothills of the Rockies. They made their way through Robert Stuart's South Pass on 8 August. By the time they reached Richard Grant's Fort Hall, provisions and morale were low. The emigrants had endured privation, disease and death as well as all the practical difficulties of travel – damaged wagons, footsore and worn-out oxen, disagreements, disease, accidents. Winter was approaching and the emigrants were anxious to re-equip for the next leg of their journey. But supplies were short at Fort Hall, and Richard Grant needed to ensure that there was enough for its needs over the winter. When Grant declined to make supplies available a group of emigrants took matters into their own hands and forced Grant to give them what they wanted.

They struggled on to Fort Walla Walla, where the commander was Archibald McKinley, but again there was little in the way of supplies, although McKinley did his best to help. Peter Burnett and others decided to make their way down the Columbia River by boat, but it proved much more hazardous than the stretch of river near the fort suggested. Several were drowned, including a 70-year old man called Alexander McClellan, two nine-year-old boys and a black woman, who was a slave belonging to Burnett. Helped by provisions sent by John McLoughlin, the survivors eventually made it to Oregon City. Peter Burnett would later move south to California and become the territory's first elected governor.

The famous Donner party of 1846 included the McCutcheon family from Missouri, William and Amanda and their child. William McCutcheon was one of those sent on ahead to Sutter's Fort to get relief for the Donner wagon train struggling through the desert. They attempted to make their way back with supplies, but blizzards made progress impossible. Amanda McCutcheon was with a group of five women and two men who were all that remained of 15 who had struggled on through snow and bitter weather, and only survived by resorting to cannibalism. The McCutcheon's baby daughter Harriet, left with the rest of the Donner party who remained camped in a mountain valley, died. Amanda McCutcheon survived the harrowing journey, and her husband William was a member of the rescue party that finally got through to find a camp of dead and dying and barely alive, the latter having kept going by consuming the former. But their ordeal was not over. There were more blizzards and more deaths. McCutcheon, six foot six and strong in spirit as well as physically, laboured heroically to keep the men, women and children going. The first historian of the Donner trek George R. Stewart (also a Scottish American) describes how McCutcheon managed to keep a fire alive as the storm raged: 'most of the children could not have long existed in the cold'.

McCutcheon himself was so chilled that as he sat by the fire he gradually charred through the four shirts that he was wearing, and did not know that he was getting warm until he felt the scorching of his skin.

Amazingly, over half of the original 89 members of the Donner party survived. William McCutcheon settled at San José and seems to have thrived. The other Scottish name among the party is that of Milton Elliot, teamster taken on by the Reed family (James and Margaret and their five children, who may also have been of Scottish origin), always described by Stewart as 'faithful Milt Elliot'. Elliot died, and provided sustenance for the desperate survivors.

The Donner tragedy was an extreme case, but most overlanders, at some stage in their journey, came close to disaster. They overloaded their wagons with furniture and other items with which to set up a new home, much of which had to be jettisoned when the going got tough. They drastically underestimated the physical demands of the journey, on themselves and their beasts. Many had minimal pioneer skills and were dependent on others when their wagons needed fixing or a child became ill. They exhausted their food supplies. James Campbell, an 1850 emigrant, came to the rescue of 'begging overlanders' who had no food.

For those who made the journey, starting from what had once been the Far West – Illinois, Iowa, Missouri perhaps, or even further east – the ordeal was not necessarily over when they reached their destination. Land claims had to be established, homes built, crops planted. Many arrived with nothing or very little. Scottish American Tabitha Moffat Brown, a widowed teacher travelling with her son and daughter and their families, set off from Missouri in 1846. On the journey she lost everything but her horse, and arrived in the Willamette valley with 6¼ cents. Eight years later, now aged 74, she owned nine town lots in Forest Grove, and lived in a handsome white frame house. There were success stories, of course, but for many the gruelling overland experience brought little real benefit.

The journey itself has become an emblem of America's pioneer spirit, fixed in our imagination by dozens of movies and fictional accounts. Andrew McLaglen's film *The Way West* (1967) is based on A.B. Guthrie's novel of the same name, the archetypal pioneer story. The movie features Robert Mitchum playing the aging mountain man and guide Dick Summers, who is a central character in Guthrie's *The Big Sky*, alongside Kirk Douglas and Richard Widmark, all familiar screen Western heroes, but it is a rather shambling interpretation of the novel. The book draws on journals and contemporary accounts and has a convincing authenticity, powerfully evoking both the landscape and the experience of travelling. The relentless effort of keeping the wheels turning runs like a chorus through the narrative. 'Drive, plod, push, tug, turn the wheels. Eat dust, damn you! Swim in sweat and freeze at night. Work the sun up. Work it down. Keep rolling.'

Guthrie's own Scottish origins are not significantly present in the novel (as they are in, for example, the work of Ivan Doig) although he gives us characters with Scottish names. Tom McBee is a disreputable and untrustworthy character, although his daughter Mercy is sweet-natured and hard-working. She is seduced by another character bearing a Scottish name, Curtis Mack. While McBee is sly and whisky-drinking and cares little for appearances, Mack is anxious to maintain an outward respectability. He is in many ways a type familiar in Scottish literature. *The Way West* portrays personal weaknesses and conflicts in the context of a vast and overwhelming landscape and a driven purpose. The emigrants are, as mountain man Dick Summers reflects, 'family men, settled with their women and easy with their children, the hard edges worn smooth, the wildness in them broke to harness. They looked ahead to farms and schools and government, to an ordered round of living.' But to achieve those things they are dependent on the few who already know the territory and whose edges are still hard.

William Chambers from Edinburgh visited the US in 1853, and recommended that Scots should not go beyond the Ohio River. 'The west may be best settled by American pioneers,' he wrote in *Things as They Are in America* (1857), 'with constitutions and habits adapted to the new regions beyond the lakes.' Although impressed by what he found in America, he took a realistic view: 'We must take America as it is, and make the best of it. It is a new, and, as yet not fully settled country; and, all things considered, has done wonders in its short progress... [generally] peopled by the more humble, or, at all events, struggling classes of European society.' His message is clear: those who voyaged to the US hoping for an easy life or a quick buck would be disappointed, and those who planned to settle on the frontier should have no illusions about the hardships they would face.

The message was not necessarily heeded. New arrivals from the old country joined the westward flow, along with second and third generation Scottish Americans. With the old Far West seeming to fill up fast – the population of Missouri almost tripled between 1830 and 1840 – the temptation was to move on, perhaps just crossing the border into the next territory. William Gilchrist, a mining engineer from Ayrshire, settled in a Kansas sod house with his wife and ten children. He would eventually become a probate judge, church elder and county commissioner. James Maclure left Indiana for Kansas in 1855, and would help to found Junction City, which marked the westward thrust of the railroad. Pioneering could be a lonely business. His wife went 18 months without seeing another woman.

The 1840s were a difficult time in much of Scotland, the consequence of potato blight, pressures on the land and on industry; emigration was encouraged. The North Texas Colonisation Company was set up in London, but among its leading members was John Alexander of Mauchline, Ayrshire. The British-American Association for Emigration and Colonisation, founded in 1841, was filled with Scots. Its president was the Duke of Argyll, its vice-presidents included the Marquess of Huntly, Lord Bute, the Earl of Dunmore, Lord Forbes, Lord Duffus, Lord Belhaven, Lord Elibank and Lord Macdonald, all major Scottish landowners with a vested interest in persuading what they regarded as surplus population to leave.

After the Civil War, the movement west, which had continued through the war years, increased exponentially, gathering up all kinds of casualties of war as well as propelling families in search of cheap land. Newly opened territories and the expanding railroads clamoured for people. There were acres and prospects for everyone, without necessarily crossing the continent:

> Come to the Garden of the West! Come to Minnesota! Come to Nebraska, the great Platte Valley. Soldiers entitled to a Homestead of 160 Acres. Purchasers, their wives and children carried free on our own elegant day coaches. Red River Valley Lands. Home-seekers! A Farm for $3 per Acre! Every Farmer, Every Farmer's Son, Every Clerk, Every Mechanic, Every Labouring Man Can Secure a Home.

The clamour was heard on the other side of the Atlantic, and in Scotland, with the war over, there was renewed interest in the land of promise: indeed, for some, the abolition of slavery made it that much more promising. The Campbells were among families who responded, father, mother and seven children. They made their way to Nebraska, where they settled in the valley of the River Platte, not far from Fort Kearney. The valley was thinly scattered with a handful of other families. The Campbells built a sod house, the only option in a territory where trees were scarce, and began the mammoth task of creating a farm out of nothing. The winter of 1865–6 was particularly severe and Mrs Campbell did not survive it. Her husband Peter carried on with the unremitting labour of ploughing and planting virgin soil, building barns, caring for stock, and raising his family.

When harvest time came the scattered community helped each other out. Peter and his eldest son were working at a neighbouring farm when news came of an Indian attack. Father and son galloped for home, but they were too late. Two older girls and four-year-old twin boys had been taken. A nine-year-old girl had managed to hide and crawl away, before running four miles to raise the alarm.

Fort Kearney had been built in 1848 as an army post along the wagon route where emigrants could stock up with supplies and trade for fresh horses and oxen. But it was not sufficiently manned to provide protection for settlers, especially at a time when the Sioux were increasingly provoked by the incursions of settlement and the activities of miners further west in Montana. Most of Peter Campbell's neighbours decided to leave, but he remained, hoping to track down and recover the missing. At first the search was fruitless. Then there was news that the children had been seen in an Oglala Sioux camp in Colorado. After negotiations, the children were bought back by the government, which is said to have paid $4,000.

During the Civil War, Missouri and Kansas were torn apart by guerilla warfare and border raids, the crucible of the James and Younger brothers (both names that could be Scottish, although Scottish origins have not been traced). When peace came, the legacy of violence lingered; nevertheless, Kansas became a more attractive proposition for homesteaders. The Buchanans, originally from Stirlingshire, settled first in Virginia. In 1867, their descendants made their way from Illinois to Kansas, 21 people with wagons, horses and mules, each wagon loaded with 1,000 pounds of supplies and equipment. At St Louis they went up the Missouri to Kansas City then loaded up the wagons again to continue their journey south to Fort Scott, near the Missouri border.

In 1862 the Homestead Act allowed those who had cultivated the same claim for five years to take ownership of the land for nothing. For others, land in the public domain was available at $1.25 per acre. Each adult US citizen was allowed 160 acres. There were many ways of circumventing the limitations, and numerous scams were operated. By the late 1880s it was beginning to look as if land was running out, and there was increasing pressure to make more available. Eyes turned towards the Indian reservations. Indian Territory, originally allocated to tribes who had been displaced from much further east and since then used as a dumping ground for others, for example the Cheyenne, was largely arid and unpromising.

It had also become an area of refuge for misfits and those on the run. Nevertheless, the land was compulsorily purchased from Indians, many of whom had been there for several generations, and made available for settlement.

Although the railroads made overland journeys infinitely faster and easier, the covered wagon was in the 1870s still the means of transport for those who had no choice but to seek unclaimed land beyond the railroad tracks and developing centres of population. In 1873 Isabella Bird, travelling alone by horseback in Colorado, encountered a wagon train making its 'dreary exodus'. She joined the emigrants for their midday meal. They had been on the road for three months, in the course of which one child and several oxen had died. There was an air of weariness and depression. They seemed, she said, 'like people on another planet' and offered a startling contrast with Denver, by that time a 'great braggart city', a major railway terminus and freight depot crowded with people and stores of all kinds.

In 1889 Indian Territory became Oklahoma, a word that means 'red earth'. On 22 April more than 50,000 people massed on the border. At the stroke of noon the race for land was on, and in 24 hours every acre had been claimed. Edna Ferber's novel *Cimarron* (1930), the basis of films by Wesley Ruggles (1931) and Anthony Mann (1960) is set in Osage, Oklahoma. Prominent in the community is Doc Nisbett, a shrewd and vinegary character whose name proclaims his Scottish origins. Nisbett has done well through land speculation, and Ferber's description makes clear both its dubious nature, and the fact that few questions were asked:

> In the rush for Territory town sites at the time of the Opening he had managed to lay his gnarled hands on five choice pieces. On these he had erected dwellings, tilted his chair up against each in turn, and took his pick of late-comers frantic for some sort of shelter they could call a home. That perjury, trickery, gun play, and murder had gone into the acquiring of these – as well as many other – sites was not considered important or, for that matter, especially interesting.

The focal point of the Oklahoma Land Race and the location of the office where land claims had to be filed was Guthrie, on the Atchison, Topeka and Santa Fe railroad. The town was named for the son of a Scottish immigrant, John Guthrie. His father William, a University of Edinburgh graduate, had left Scotland for Indiana, where John grew up to become a lawyer. He gave his name to the town through his involvement with the railroad, which was laying track through Indian Territory in 1876–7.

Every Scottish name on the map of the American West has a tale to tell. North Dakota saw the arrival of many Scots, some coming across the border from Canada. Kintyre was founded by the Campbell family, echoing a part of Scotland where Campbells are prominent. They were cattle and sheep ranchers. Other Scottish names in the Dakotas include Finley, Abercrombie, Kenmore, Dunseith, Aberdeen, McIntosh, McLaughlin and Murdo.

With the end of the Civil War the building of railroads to carry people and freight west re-commenced. The journey was transformed, at least as far as those towns on the railroad lines. But settlement could still be a difficult business, demanding backbreaking work, loneliness and disappointment. Homesteaders often did not stay long where they first planted themselves. The Stewart family, moving from Virginia to Illinois to Iowa, from where the menfolk lit out for the California gold fields, is a good example. The dream of somewhere better and kinder was remarkably robust.

Granville Stuart had travelled west with his father and brother in 1852. More than half a century later he was in a train, following the course of the North Platte River, on the same route he had taken with wagons and horses. Then, they had dealt with quicksands, storms and cholera, and had met a young woman and her four young children coming towards them in a light wagon. Her husband had died on the trail, and she was trying to return to Illinois. In 1907 Stuart was travelling in 'a luxurious car of the Union Pacific Railroad', looking out on:

... what was once a lonely stretch of plains, occupied by highly cultivated farms and fine residences, the owners of which were entirely unconscious that there were few fields bordering the view that did not have several unknown graves in them, where rested the bones of hardy pioneers who fell by the wayside, when on their way to form a western empire on the shores of the far distant Pacific ocean.

CHAPTER 5

Cowboys

Whoopee ti yi yo, git along little dogies,
It's your misfortune and none of my own.
Whoopee ti yi yo, git along little dogies,
For you know Wyoming will be your new home.

'*Whoopee ti yi yo*', traditional, sung by Woody Guthrie

IN 1874 A YOUNG MAN from Kelso in the Scottish Borders travelled by train to Denver, Colorado, through country that 'opened up new visions'. It was, he said, 'a fast-moving picture that passed before my eyes', and went on:

> The Indian receding into the distance; the trapper period also fading away; the 49ers, a halo of romance hanging 'round their struggles and exploits; the discovery of gold in Colorado in 1859; the slow, measured step of bridling streams, while the cowman and his fantastic help added endless stories, adventures by flood, field, and mountain to an already overcharged volcano.

The young man was John Clay, and he would play a part in the adventures of the cowman, but at this stage he was only looking around him. He was from an agricultural and stock-breeding background, but was dissatisfied with prospects at home. He was impatient with the limits imposed by class and sought a less restricted environment. 'Inheriting from my parents many radical views, mainly political,' he wrote in his memoir *My Life on the Range* (1924), 'and being naturally blessed with independence and self-reliance, it was a short step to explore the widening influence of the new world.' Five years after his first visit, he was back in

North America, spending time in Canada and California before settling in Wyoming. It was 1879, and the beef bonanza was gaining momentum. Many Scots, and a great deal of Scottish money, would be involved.

Two years earlier *The Scotsman* newspaper had sent James Macdonald to the United States to investigate the cattle industry. Cheap American beef was flooding into Britain, and there was concern that this would undermine local production. Macdonald's trip was followed by a Royal Commission, which reported enthusiastically on the potential of raising cattle in the prairies. Cattle ranges were in effect free, and as long as a source of water could be controlled vast herds of cattle could be run on them. Though the report said nothing to reassure British farmers, it alerted the country to the possibility of massive profits from American cows. The message was received with particular enthusiasm by Scots.

Others crossed the Atlantic to see for themselves, among them the Earl of Airlie, who was already chairman of the Scottish American Mortgage Company. The American cattle industry needed investment and it needed to improve its stock. Scots had both the money and the know-how. The result was the creation of Scottish-owned ranches in the cattle-range states and the contribution of many Scots to the practical business of ranching. John Clay's role was, initially, to advise potential investors on what they would get for their money. The counting of stock was an inexact science, and with cattle roaming freely over vast areas there was plenty of opportunity for both error and deliberate subterfuge. Scottish investors in Edinburgh and Dundee, who would never see the places and the beasts that were the source of profit, needed people they could trust on the ground.

There were already Scottish Americans involved in ranching, in Texas and the southwest. One if the earliest was John Simpson Chisum (the name mutated from Chisholm and he may have been related to Jesse of the Chisholm Trail) who was county clerk of Lamar County, Texas, before moving into the cattle business. During the Civil War he took advantage of the demand for beef by driving cattle to Shreveport on the Mississippi for shipment east, and set up a meatpacking business at Fort Smith, Arkansas. His ranching activities began when he agreed to manage a ranch on the site of what is now Fort Worth in return for a share of the profits. Later, he moved to New Mexico, where his three brothers joined him on the Jingle-Bob Ranch in Lincoln County. Chisum was hard-headed and possibly unscrupulous. A degree of ruthlessness was perhaps necessary, but he seems to have been engaged in a number of dubious business deals, in particular an episode in which he undertook to market cattle for several Texas ranchers who never saw their money.

In the years following the Civil War Lincoln County was plagued by Mescalero Apaches on cattle-thieving raids. Chisum took matters into his own hands by organising a reprisal. A band of armed men rode to the Mescalero reservation and, having first got the agents drunk, killed a large number of Indians. Apaches were not the only rustlers. By the late 1870s rustling was widespread, and it triggered eruptions of violence, including the series of incidents that came to be known as the Lincoln County War. Things got so out of hand that the president was called on to intervene (see Chapter 9).

While John Chisum was battling with rustlers, Henry Campbell was initiating what would become one of the most successful cattle enterprises of this period. In 1840 Campbell had arrived in Texas with his parents. He fought in the Civil War, and in 1869 was hired to drive a herd of cattle to California, but drought forced him to abandon the drive in Nevada, and sell the beasts. Despite this setback, he undertook cattle drives to New Orleans and Dodge City, responding to the growing demand for beef, and he started to build up his own herd. Chicago was the focal point of the meat market, and a visit there in 1878 to sell his cattle brought him together with Colonel Alfred Markham Britton, keen to put money into cows. With Britton's money and Campbell's experience, a new cattle company was formed. Land was acquired in the Texas Panhandle, and Campbell managed the ranch. Three years later Britton and

Campbell sold their herd to the newly formed Matador Land and Cattle Company, financed largely from Dundee. Robert Fleming, on the company's board, went out to Texas and acquired 300,000 acres of Panhandle land and 60,000 head of cattle. He appointed Henry Campbell as manager.

The Matador was only one of many cattle enterprises owned and directed by Scots, most of whom never set eyes on a longhorn cow, knew little of what ranching involved, and in some cases were uncharacteristically susceptible to the hyperbole of cattle company prospectuses. It seemed that everyone with cash to spare wanted to have a slice of the bonanza. The Prairie Cattle Company was registered in 1880, based in Edinburgh. It soon had land in New Mexico and Colorado as well as the Panhandle; for a time it was running its cattle on an unbroken range stretching from the Canadian River in Texas to the Arkansas River in Colorado. A year later came the Texas Land and Cattle Company, registered like the Matador in Dundee. Its success encouraged investment in the Matador; Robert Fleming was on the board of both companies. The Cattle Ranche and Land Company was sold to Scots in 1883 – John Clay advised on the sale, as he did on the affairs of the Rocking Chair Ranch acquired by a Scottish group in the same year.

In Scotland, Matador affairs were under the watchful eye of Alexander Mackay, chartered accountant and one of the board secretaries. John Clay, who came to know most of the Scots involved in the cattle business, thought highly of him. In Texas, from 1890, another Scot kept an equally watchful eye on the day-to-day business of ranching. He was Murdo Mackenzie, born near Tain, Easter Ross, in 1850. He came to the United States with plenty of useful experience, having begun his career as a bank clerk and acquired some training in the law before managing the Balnagown estate of Sir Charles Ross, which sustained 200 tenant farms and 12,000 sheep, as well as 9,000 acres set aside for game. Mackenzie was a year with the Prairie Cattle Company before in 1891 taking on the Matador, where he soon gained a formidable reputation.

Lewis Atherton, historian of cattle ranching, describes him as 'probably the greatest of all ranch managers'. He equally impressed John Clay, who writes of 'dear, clever Murdo', whose appointment as the Matador's manager was a 'masterstroke'. Mackenzie, who was both progressive and practical, 'touched with a magic hand the whole situation'.

Mackenzie dealt calmly with emergencies – his life was threatened on at least two occasions. He preferred not to carry a gun, but did sanction vigilante action against cattle thieves. He was a tough negotiator, and fought for improved rates on the railroads and against the stranglehold of the Chicago meat packers. And he banned drinking and gambling among his employees, hard to credit in the context of the portrayal in Westerns of off-duty cowboys. One of his sons, Dode, conformed more to the stereotype. He worked on the Matador's northern ranges, but his life came to an abrupt end when, threatening to kill a bartender who refused to sell him another drink, he was himself shot.

Mackenzie and his Scottish wife Isabella McBain ran operations from Trinidad, Colorado, where, according to Atherton, 'they maintained much the same way of life that the family had known in Scotland', which included Murdo playing the fiddle. From 1904–11 he was president of the American National Livestock Corporation, and he became a good friend of Theodore Roosevelt. In 1912 he left the Matador to become a ranch manager in Brazil, but returned seven years later when his successor died. His son John became assistant manager of the Matador in 1947, eight years after his father's death, and then headed the US office until the company was sold in 1951.

When Mackenzie took over as ranch manager the short-lived beef bonanza was on its way out. Cattle ranching never again reached the heights of the early 1880s, which had sparked the enthusiasm of normally cautious Scots in Edinburgh and Dundee. By the time James Tait published in Edinburgh his influential pamphlet *The Cattle Fields of the Far West* (1884), the industry was running into difficulties. His message was that cattle grazed on the vast western ranges could be left to forage for themselves, 'with the expenditure of a minimum of care and outlay on the part of the owners'. The future of the cattle trade was, he said, 'luminous with promise'. Tait himself was involved in a number of land and ranching projects in the West, without success. He also tried his hand at writing fiction and at publishing, but he died in obscurity in 1917.

A closer look would have revealed ominous signs. Both the Cattle Ranche and Land Company and the Rocking Chair Ranch were in difficulties. The former had sold range rights to the Scots for £50,000, but range rights were an illusive concept in a situation where proprietorship was assumed rather than assigned. Settlers were making land claims which ate into the open range. Cattle counts were problematic and dodgy deals hard to trace. It was difficult for owners 5,000 miles away to know what was going on.

The principal shareholders of the Rocking Chair Ranch were James Gordon, Earl of Aberdeen, and Edward Marjoribanks, Lord Tweedmouth, who was a governor of the Commercial Bank of Scotland. The ranch was inefficiently run and haemorrhaged cattle to rustlers. Lord Tweedmouth dispatched his son Archie to sort things out, who duly arrived bringing his own horses. The Rocking Chair cowboys, who called it 'Nobility Ranch', were not impressed. British horses, flat saddles and the British style of riding were of little use for herding and cutting out cattle, roping and branding. Eventually, Lords Aberdeen and Tweedmouth themselves arrived to find out what was happening to their cattle, but they were not sharp enough to spot that the ranch manager was counting the same herd several times. When the owners eventually sold the ranch there were 14,000 head on the books, and 300 at the final roundup.

The Espuela Cattle Company of Texas was bought by a Scottish syndicate in 1883, and became the Spur Ranch. It attracted investors mainly from Aberdeen, and an influential member of the board was Robert Burnett, Aberdeen's land surveyor and a director of the Caledonian Railways. The company purchased alternate sections of land in the Texas public domain, and leased the land in between, a canny move which allowed them to fence the whole area. Fencing the range was made practicable by the introduction of barbed wire, patented in 1873, and it changed the working practice of the cowboy. Now instead of riding herd on unconfined cattle a key task was line riding – checking that mile upon mile of fencing remained intact – lonelier and more tedious.

The manager of the Spur Ranch was Spottswood Lomax, of likely Scottish origin though born in Virginia – 'tall, slender, sociable, soft-spoken, polished, educated, and widely travelled' according to Lewis Atherton. But he was also somewhat remote – his wife preferred to live in Fort Worth rather than on the ranch – and although his cowboys, like most others, worked a seven-day week the outfit suffered from hard times in the later 1880s. Lomax's salary was reduced. In 1889 he left the Spur and Fred Horsbrugh took over as manager. He had been sent out from Scotland three years earlier to look after the company's investments, and in the intervening period had gained direct experience of the cattle industry. He remained manager of the Spur until 1904.

The largest ranch in the Texas Panhandle was the XIT. Its first manager was B.H. Campbell, who had been a cattleman in Indian Territory before taking on the job, but although experienced he was neither efficient nor trustworthy. In a deal with his cousin, from which both gained financially, he arranged for inferior cattle to be purchased. He was building up his own herd at the same time as being responsible for the XIT cattle, and took much more care with his own beasts than with those of his employers. In spite of the XIT hiring Texas Rangers to police the range, rustling increased, and when in 1887 the owners sent an agent to investigate, he found known outlaws among the workforce.

Scottish investment was directed into ambitious schemes involving thousands of acres of land and thousands of head of cattle. But not all ranching and not all Scottish involvement were on such a scale. In 1879 the 27-year-old Robert Cunninghame Graham disembarked at New Orleans with his Chilean wife Gabriela and a plan to breed mules at Brownsville on the Texas–Mexico border. Although born in London, his family came from Stirlingshire, and he was unequivocally a Scot, as his later political career would demonstrate – he was co-founder of the National Party of Scotland. By the time he arrived in New Orleans he had already lived in South America for seven years, where he spent much of the time in Argentina and Uruguay acquiring skills as a horseman and cattle drover.

Cunninghame Graham quickly abandoned his original plan and left Brownsville after two weeks. He and Gabriela moved on to Corpus Christi, but there the lawlessness that made them leave Brownsville was even worse. 'Every day there are one or two [killings],' he commented in a letter, 'such a thing as a fair fight is unknown.' They changed their plans again, and went to San Antonio, 'by far the most picturesque place in Texas', with the ruined Alamo at its centre. In a letter written half a century later he gave a picture of life there:

> I used to unsaddle always at the Buffalo Camp and then make my way to the Menger Hotel, where I had a trunk of store clothes. Then, I fancy, there would be a schooner of beer, a cocktail or a whisky straight, for Texas was a free country in those days, and certainly a thirsty land... They were the days of the Mexican freighters, buffalo hunters, cowmen, and other worthies of whom the world was not worthy...

Cunninghame Graham did not stay long in Texas, but was remarkably active. He and Gabriela took a wagon train of cotton to San Luis Potosí in Mexico, a journey that was long, difficult and dangerous. As well as bad roads, bandits, a parched landscape and many discomforts, there were Indian attacks: 'we had a brush with Lipan Apaches, but beat them off, after forming the wagons into a corral, just as you may see in the film The Covered Wagon'. (*The Covered Wagon*, directed by James Cruze in 1923, was the first epic Western.) They returned to Texas, and in 1880 Cunninghame Graham went into a ranching partnership with a Mexican Greek. But the venture was short-lived. He returned from a business trip to find the ranch had been destroyed by Apaches and the stock gone. All his money had been invested in the ranch.

It wasn't quite the end of his US career as over the next few months he participated in cattle drives and buffalo hunts, which took him to Mexico, New Mexico and Arizona; on one of his trips he met William Cody, aka Buffalo Bill. But in 1881 the Cunninghame Grahams gave up their Texas adventure and returned to Europe. It was not a success story, although it furnished both of them with experiences that fed their writing. When his father died in 1883, Cunninghame Graham took over the debt-ridden family estates in Dunbartonshire, and went on to have an influential career as writer and politician.

Like so many others, the Cunninghame Grahams were attracted to Texas by the prospect of easy money from ranching. Robert's seven years in South America ensured that he had the skills and the enthusiasm for the job, but they were not enough. For the benefit of potential investors in Scotland, the impact of Indian raids and a host of other difficulties were underplayed. If those who actually went to the American West to acquire first-hand knowledge of the situation were aware of the hazards, they were not keen to report that, for example, criminality and carelessness could eat into profits. It soon became apparent that the climate was also a factor. Serious drought and severe winters put an end to many ranchers' dreams.

By the early 1880s the focus was beginning to shift from the south west to territories further north. In 1882 Alexander Swan, who grew up on a farm in Pennsylvania, visited Scotland looking for buyers for his Swan Land and Cattle Company, which owned a large ranch in south eastern Wyoming along the Laramie, Chug and Sybille Rivers. By the late 1870s the rich grazing available on public land in Wyoming and Montana was attracting Texas ranchers, and herds were driven north to fatten on the abundant grass before being sent to market. Ernest Haycox in his novel *Free Grass* (1958) captures the epic nature of the journey; the rivers crossed marking the progress northwards:

> Twenty-five hundred cattle trampling a broad trail across the lush earth... Hot sun beating down; swift spring rains pouring out of the sky, flooding the coulees and vanishing as quickly as they came. And again the hot sun playing on the wet prairies and the steam rising up. Five miles a day, eight miles a day, sometimes 15 miles a day. They crossed the ford of the Smoky Hill, they crossed the Saline and the Solomon. Kansas was behind, and the plains of Nebraska beckoned them north – level, limitless.

Such treks were the prelude to the spread of serious cattle ranching to the north, made easier by the coming of the railroad. As in Texas, much Scottish money was involved, and many Scots and Scottish Americans were prominent in the Wyoming and Montana cattle business. In the final episode of the *Lonesome Dove* television series, Gus McCrae (although he does not survive the journey) and his fellow cowboys drive a herd of cattle from Texas to Montana. In the sequel, *Return to Lonesome Dove*, Woodrow Coll makes the same journey with a herd of horses. His unscrupulous Montana neighbour is a Scot partial to single malt whisky who has called his ranch 'Kenilworth' (after Walter Scott's novel).

Alexander Swan had no difficulty finding buyers for his company, and it remained in Scottish ownership for over 40 years. The ranch, however, had mixed fortunes, and there were conflicting views of Swan himself. Based in Cheyenne, where he had a 'fine home', was a stalwart of the Cheyenne Club and the local opera house, and supported the Presbyterian Church, he was held in high regard by those in Scotland. At the 1883 shareholders' meeting, George Prentiss voiced his approbation: 'The whole way from Chicago to Cheyenne Mr Swan is well known on the road as anyone who travels on it; and you never hear his name mentioned without an encomium passed upon him.' Swan himself owned 4,000 acres of land in Iowa, where he ran 1,500 head of cattle and horses, was president of the South Omaha Land Syndicate, and served in the legislatures of both Iowa and Wyoming. His daughter Louise was sent to Europe for her schooling. But in 1892 the Swan Land and Cattle Company went bankrupt and he was dismissed as general manager. The Scottish investors incurred heavy losses. Swan, who would eventually die in an asylum in Ogden, Utah, was succeeded by John Clay.

Clay was highly critical of Swan. In 1883, when he sold the company to the Scots, he was heavily in debt and the cattle count was not verified. Clay's comment on Swan was, 'I doubt, so far as the range is concerned, if he ever owned an honest dollar.' He was, according to Clay, over-ambitious, vain and overbearing. 'His rise was meteoric, his fall terrific.' There are many other Wyoming tales of an uncharacteristic Scottish lack of caution when it came to investing in cattle ranching. Another Scottish purchase was the Seventy-one Quarter Circle Ranch on the Sweetwater near Rawlins, managed by John Stewart. John Clay was again asked to investigate the problem, when the actual cattle count proved far lower than stated on paper.

Clay has left a vivid description of John Stewart, who had a wholesale grocery business in Council Bluffs as well as a ranch:

> He had a strong face, rather spoiled by a shifty eye, but all over he had the marks of strong tenacity, full of enterprise and aggressive push. There was the air of a successful man about him. He was an interesting talker, unfolding gradually his plans and policies, and how in the rough-and-tumble days of frontier life he had reached an era of easy independence.

Clay clearly had some admiration for this Ulster Scot, although he was aware that Stewart had an eye to the main chance. If over-enthusiastic buyers were prepared to accept figures that did not involve gathering and re-branding the cattle, a laborious and expensive task, Clay was not going to blame the ranchers. 'John T. Stewart saw his opportunity to unload while the boom was still expanding,' was his comment, and he added, 'Small blame to him.'

Scots rose to the bait. Among those who on 22 June 1882 gathered in the Frederick Street, Edinburgh office of Graham, Johnston and Fleming were Thomas Nelson, publisher, Archibald Coats of the Paisley thread firm J. & P. Coats, W.J. Menzies, WS, Andrew Thomson, timber merchant, Mr Gifford, cashier of the National Bank of Scotland, James Ford of Leith, Alexander Gibson of Belgrave Crescent, Edinburgh and J.D. Lawrie of Monkrigg. Also present was James Tait, whose 1884 pamphlet would help to overheat the Scottish enthusiasm for American cattle. The meeting agreed to form the Wyoming Cattle Ranche Company and to acquire John Stewart's ranch, which covered an area of 4,000 square miles, including 4,000 acres of 'fenced meadow land', with 19,000 head of cattle and 150 horses, as well as buildings and equipment. The description in the prospectus of Wyoming range country explains the attraction of the proposition:

> Wyoming is termed the 'Bonanza' Cattle territory, and Cattle are driven to it from every pastoral district in the Union, even from a distance of twelve to fifteen hundred miles. Here they attain the maximum of growth and fat, and the perfection of quality ... and when fattened they are already within the area of the market... The Union Pacific Railway intersects the property, and that company's station at Rawlins is immediately contiguous, thus affording ready access to the chief cattle centres at Chicago and elsewhere.

The prospectus included an extract from an article written by Wyoming's governor, extolling the territory as 'a pastoral region without parallel'.

It must have been hard for the gentlemen gathered in the Frederick Street office to imagine a country so very different from the small fields and bleak uplands of Scotland. In the 1880s, when thousands of Scottish acres were talked of, it was in the context of grouse moors and deer forests. The notion of huge tracts of land being suitable for raising cattle, or even sheep, was entirely foreign. Perhaps it was not surprising that they got carried away. Inevitably, chickens came home to roost and, not long after, Clay found himself being asked by the Scottish owners to investigate the business managed by Stewart. The case went to court, and while the Scottish owners won they received only a third of the money they claimed.

The potential of the Wyoming grasslands was recognised at an early stage. The Stock Growers' Association, based in Cheyenne, was founded in 1873, and Scots were prominent among its members. Among Scottish names that appear in a list drawn up by John Clay are Anderson, Baxter, Blair, Bowie, Campbell, Christie, Gilchrist, Graham, Guthrie, Hanna, Hay, McFarlane, Rankin, Robertson and Simpson. Clay himself was a leading figure in the association. The Montana Livestock Association included the names Crawford, Graham, Irvine, Lang, McDowell, Maxwell, Ramsay, Robertson, Ross, Scott and Stuart among its members. Place names such as Douglas, Lamont and Sinclair in Wyoming, and Glasgow, Forsyth and Hamilton in Montana also signify a Scottish imprint. There was a concentration of Scots settled in the Wind River area in the west of Wyoming; the East Fork of the Wind River was known as 'Little Scotland'. At Lander, tucked under the Wind River mountain range, were to be found McDonalds, Findlays, Finlaysons, Murrays, Brodies and other Scottish families. The first governor of Wyoming was John A. Campbell.

Granville Stuart became involved in the cattle business in 1879. His wanderings had taken him from Illinois to Iowa to California to Montana, where he recognised the potential for raising cattle. After some months of searching, he and his partners selected a stretch of land along the Judith River, a tributary of the Upper Missouri overlooked by the Judith Mountains. It was, Stuart believed, 'an ideal cattle range' and it was there for the taking: 'None of this land is surveyed and the only way to hold it is by occupying it.' He built houses, stables and a corral, and fenced 1,000 acres for hay. The plan was to supply beef to nearby Fort Maginnis, but this arrangement took some time to set up. There were other difficulties. Cree from across the Canadian border helped themselves to cattle. The severe winters meant that range riders had to be out in often appalling conditions to check stock. In 1880–1 there were blizzards right through from December to May: 'The range looked and felt like the Arctic regions,' was Stuart's comment. In the circumstances he did well to lose only 13 per cent of his stock. Worse winters were to come.

The annual spring round up was a time of intensive activity. Stuart and neighbouring ranchers collaborated to gather, identify and brand cattle. The 12 ranches on the Fort Maginnes range included those run by Robert Coburn, N.W. McCaulley, C.D. Duncan, Robert Hamilton, James Fergus, William Burnett and J.L. Stuart (Granville's brother), all suggesting a Scottish origin. It could take as long as six weeks to gather in the cattle, and then thousands of head had to be sorted and separated. Stuart vividly describes the scene of departure at the start of the round-up.

> Early in the morning the big horse herd would be driven in and each man would catch and saddle his mount. There was a number of horses that would buck and a lot of half-broken colts to ride that would cause a certain amount of excitement. The horse herder in charge of the horse wranglers would lead off in the direction of the objective corral followed by the white-covered four-horse chuck wagons, and then the troop of cowboys with their gay handkerchiefs, fine saddles, and silver-mounted bridles and spurs.

Often there was a dance the night before the round-up commenced, the exuberance of the cowboys undeterred by a dearth of female partners.

When the cattle were brought in, there followed 'hard and fast' work in the corrals. 'The dust and heat and smell of singeing hair was stifling while the bellowing of the cattle was a perfect bedlam.' In the autumn there was the calf round-up, and then a gathering of the cattle to be sent to market. For Stuart this involved a 120-mile drive to Custer, where the beasts were loaded onto the Northern Pacific Railroad for transport east. In the autumn of 1883 they were camped on a branch of McDonald Creek, on their way to Custer. The weather was bad, rain and early snow, and something spooked the cattle. In seconds, the cowboys had a stampede on their hands:

> The tramping of flying hooves and rattling horns sounded like artillery. The herders were with the stampede in an instant and in an instant every man was in the saddle after them. The night was pitch dark and there was nothing to guide us but the thunder of hoofs... Through the rain and the mud and pitch dark, up and down banks and over broken ground, they all went in a mad rush.

Finally the cowboys succeeded in getting the herd to mill and the frightened animals were calmed. By the time all the stragglers had been recovered, some of the men had been in the saddle for 24 hours.

Stuart had great respect for many of his fellow ranchers and for the resilience and toughness of the cowboys. William Burnett, he said, was 'the best range foreman that I ever met'. The cowboys' work was 'steady, hard, and hazardous', and they compensated for months of unremitting and often isolated labour by drinking and gambling when they got the chance. They also 'liked a good show and a dance' and were partial to tinned oysters and ice cream, which occasionally relieved a diet of beans, bacon, beef, bread and coffee.

Stuart's description of cowboys with their fine saddles, silver-mounted gear, pearl-handled six-shooters and stylish cartridge belts, rattlesnake hat bands and brightly coloured silk handkerchiefs, provides a template for the cowboy's image in film and fiction. His comments on cowboy behaviour also contribute:

> Always on the frontier beyond organised society or law, they formulated laws of their own that met their requirements, and they enforced them, if necessary, at the point of a six-shooter. They were reluctant to obey any law but their own and chafed under restraint. They were loyal to their outfit and to one another... A shooting scrape that resulted in the death of one or both of the combatants was not considered a murder but an affair between themselves.

Stuart's memoirs were published in 1925, by which time the cowboy as an iconic hero had been known to a wide public for several decades, and his portrayals may be touched by romance, but the core of his descriptions of ranching activity is authentic.

Stuart, like all the Montana and Wyoming ranchers, was severely hit by the winters of 1885–6 and 1886–7, in which blizzards, drifting snow and unremitting cold killed thousands of cattle. When the snow finally melted the full extent of the ranchers' losses was revealed, with carcasses visible everywhere. It was, Stuart wrote, 'the death knell to the cattle range business on anything like the scale it had been run on before'. It was a sombre time for ranchers on the northern ranges. 'A business that had been fascinating to me before became distasteful,' said Stuart. 'I never wanted to own again an animal that I could not feed and shelter.' It was a hard lesson for ranchers, who had to come to terms with the need for cattle to be cared for during the winter. Many never recovered from their losses. The lean and rugged Texas longhorn was by this time being improved by stock imported from Britain, to produce more and better beef, but the result was less hardy animals. Scots, including John Clay, played a leading role in the import of cattle, sheep and horses into North America.

To the east in the Dakotas the consequences of those cruel winters were equally devastating. In the late 1870s and early 1880s ranchers and farmers were beginning to get established in the Dakotas, which attracted a number of Scots from Canada as well as Scottish Americans. Among the latter was Gregor Lang, an Ulster Scot who crossed the Atlantic to find out for himself if the United States was indeed the land of the free. He brought with him ideas absorbed from Tom Paine and other radicals, and as a staunch Democrat was rather an unusual figure among Dakota ranchers. His nearest neighbour was Theodore Roosevelt, who was politically as well as physically on the other side of the fence. The frontier appealed to Gregor Lang because it seemed to offer an environment of political and social freedom, but he soon discovered that black, Native and

Hispanic Americans were seen as less equal than others. He, his wife and his son Lincoln ignored distinctions of class and race, and were criticised for their attitudes. Mrs Lang fed destitute Indians, of which there were growing numbers as reservation land was whittled away.

The Langs arrived in 1883, straight from Northern Ireland, and settled near Medora in the Dakota Badlands. Lincoln was 16 years old, and although he took time to adapt to the rigours of pioneer life, he later wrote about that part of the frontier with appreciation: 'A wild romantic rock-garden of the Gods where in peace and security the wild and untamed reveled in the exalted atmosphere with which nature had surrounded them.' The Langs soon experienced the changes that affected all the ranchers. It wasn't just hard winters that brought them up against some tough realities. As more and more cattle and cattlemen poured north, the abundant grass was overgrazed and animals faced the winter without enough fat on them to survive. Excessive trapping of beaver dried up the streams – the beaver dams helped to contain the water – and pressure on land increased. When the Langs first settled there were only a few scattered ranches, but even in 1883 they had to give up their initial claim to an outfit arriving with a large herd of cattle from the south. (They declined to fight for it, though claim jumping often triggered violence, and is the theme of many Westerns.) By the end of the decade there were no easy profits in cattle any more. Gregor Lang eventually left Dakota and the United States, and spent his last years in Edinburgh.

According to John Leakey (in his book *The West that Was, from Texas to Montana*, 1958) two of the biggest ranchers in North Dakota were Gene Buchanan, 'a feisty sort of fellow', and Jim Drummond. Leakey's account of Dakota ranching is well populated with Scottish names. Jim Oliphant and Jack McDonald were cowboys (McDonald a suspected rustler), and Angus Kennedy was prominent in the cattlemen's association. Another Kennedy, John, was a local sheriff.

It has been suggested that centuries of cattle droving in the Scottish Highlands and Borders gave Scots a natural affinity for the American cattle business. Scottish names are found not just among the ranch owners and managers, but also among the cowhands who worked the cattle, and the horse wranglers, and the drifters who might spend a season on a ranch before moving on wherever else they could earn a few dollars, and the cooks who were so essential to ranching morale. Billy Irvine, mixed-blood son of a Scots fur trader, was a cowhand in Montana and Wyoming. When in 1900 Murdo MacLean from Wester Ross arrived in Billings, Montana, he signed up as a cowboy along with other Scots. The hotel they stayed in was run by Gaelic speakers. Edgar Bronson in his *Reminiscences of a Ranchman* (1908) remembers Red Cameron, cook at the Wyoming ranch where Bronson had his first cowpunching job. The way Bronson reproduces Cameron's speech makes it clear that he was not long out of Scotland. His comment when Bronson narrowly escaped being gored by an incensed heifer was: 'Gi'n ye had as muckle sense as luck, ye'd get yer eemortality in this wurrld, by livin' forever!'

John Clay had no illusions about the life or the character of the cowboy. If frontier life was 'free ... with little restraint', it bred a tough independence which had little of romance in it. The cow-punchers in the Sweetwater region were 'the real simon-pure, devil-may-care, roistering, gambling, immoral, revolver-heeled, brazen, light-fingered lot'. Their life and the realities of the cattle business were a long way from the 'cozy corners of Scotch cities' where much of the money that paid them originated.

CHAPTER 6

Prairie Sod and Mountain Pasture

I plant my seed in the new dug ground
And I'm living in the light of the morning.

'New Found Land', Woody Guthrie

WHEN BROTHERS John and David Muir left Dunbar on Scotland's east coast to travel with their father by train to Glasgow and then to sail 'away from beloved Scotland', they were full of enthusiasm. It was 1849:

> We could not know then what we were leaving, what we were to encounter in the New World, nor what our gains were likely to be. We were too young and full of hope for fear or regret, but not too young to look forward with eager enthusiasm to the wonderful schoolless bookless American wilderness.

The voyage to New York took six weeks; from there they made their way to Buffalo. The original plan was to settle in Canada, but hearing that good land was available in Wisconsin they changed direction. Their destination was 'the border of the settled part of the country', where Daniel Muir acquired a quarter-section, built a shanty, and set about clearing and planting the land.

Wisconsin is east of the Mississippi. By 1849 thousands of pioneers were looking beyond it to the new Far West, and were plodding across the arid plains and the savage mountains, pulled by a vision of fertile valleys inviting the plough. Tales of the wonderful fertility of, for example, Oregon's Willamette valley, were a powerful attraction. They permeate the accounts of the wagon trains, in both fact and fiction. A.B. Guthrie in his novel *The Way West* depicts the magnetism, strong enough to pull the emigrants onwards and to bind them more or less together in the face of huge difficulties and personality clashes. 'Everyone talking about Oregon,' says Rebecca Evans at the beginning of the book, and her husband Lije is convinced that the green Willamette valley is the dream destination: 'Take climate ... or water power or health or timber or soil or convenience to markets, Oregon beats them all.'

But territories such as Wisconsin, Iowa and Minnesota remained the goal of many emigrants. A few years after the Muirs started their new life not far from Portage on the Wisconsin River, Laurence Oliphant was in Minnesota, immediately to the west, and found virgin country inviting settlement:

> The aspect of the country generally was tempting to the settler ... Well-wooded hills, and valleys, and meadows with long rich grass, bore testimony to the richness of the soil, while lakes sparkled in the sunshine, and formed a most attractive picture; and I could not but believe that this country, which looked so bright and smiling even in a state of savage nature, was only waiting for the hand of man still more to gladden and to beautify it.

Although Oliphant found 'a state of savage nature', Scots had been settling in Minnesota since the 1830s, and continued to be attracted there over the next decades. Some came over the border from Canada. Scottish mortgage companies encouraged settlement in Minnesota and neighbouring Iowa, as well as further west, through the offer of loans on attractive terms. The Dundee Land Investment Company purchased two Minnesota town sites, named Airlie and Dundee, with the aim of encouraging Scottish emigrants to purchase land on an installment plan. There was significant Scottish settlement in Iowa, where one of the territory's earliest settlers was another Muir, Samuel (no relation so far as is known), who was a graduate of Edinburgh University.

The Scots who arrived in North America to take up land grants developed a relationship to the land that was different from what most had experienced in the old country. For a start, the land was theirs. Most of the farmers and crofters who left Scotland had no prospect of owning the land they worked. In many cases, the acres of their tenancies were not sufficient for subsistence. They may have been split many times between members of families. This, as much as eviction by landlords replacing people with sheep or reserves for deer and grouse shooting, was a reason for leaving. The scale of the new territory was another striking difference, not just overall but in terms of the acreage settlers found themselves farming. A quarter-section, 160 acres, which is what the Homestead Act of 1862 specified, was unimaginable for Highland crofters used to cultivating fragments of over-worked land and keeping a few cattle on mountain shielings in the summer and with virtually nothing in the winter. Even for Lowland tenant farmers that kind of acreage was unusual. And many Scots with no farming experience arrived in the US to take up land claims. For them, the challenge of getting to grips with land that had never been tilled was huge.

Daniel Muir was neither a Highlander nor a farmer, and Wisconsin was neither the prairies nor the mountains. But his son John's account of homesteading in the 1850s, in *My Boyhood and Youth* (1913), gives a vivid impression of what was involved in survival as a pioneer farmer. As an 11-year-old he had relished the prospect of no school, but although he and his brother had time to revel in the wilderness they were expected to work relentlessly hard on the land. He was ploughing at the age of 12, 'when my head reached but little above the handles', walking barefoot in the furrows. Stumps had to be cleared: 'it was dull, hard work leaning over on my knees all day, chopping out those tough oak and hickory stumps, deep down below the crowns of the big roots'. The crops had to be hoed. Then came the back-breaking weeks of the harvest, cutting, raking and binding, stacking and thrashing, working 16 or 17 hours a day. There was no let up on the chores: feeding the cattle and horses, chopping firewood, carrying water from the spring, fencing, 'shelling corn, fanning wheat, thrashing with the flail, making axe-handles or ox-yokes, mending things, or sprouting and sorting potatoes in the cellar'.

It was, John Muir argued decades later, 'over-industrious' work, which made slaves of the homesteaders. 'The fat folk grew lean and the lean leaner, while the rosy cheeks brought from Scotland and other cool countries across the sea faded to yellow like the wheat.' None of the community was so 'excessively industrious' as Daniel Muir, 'though nearly all of the Scotch, English, and Irish worked too hard, trying to make good homes and to lay up money enough for comfortable independence'.

When the Muirs first settled on their farm, their nearest neighbour was four miles away. But within a few years, 'almost every quarter-section of government land was taken up, mostly by enthusiastic home-seekers from Great Britain', including many Scots. But there were also Americans, 'drifting indefinitely westward in covered wagons, seeking their fortunes like winged seeds'.

> The axe and the plough were kept very busy; cattle, horses, sheep, and pigs multiplied; barns and corn-cribs were filled up, and man and beast were well fed; a schoolhouse was built, which was used also for a church; and in a very short time the new country began to look like the old one.

For those used to working land that had been cultivated for hundreds of years, the prospect of virgin soil was enticing. Even families who had been farming for only a generation or two in the eastern States could not resist the lure of land that had never been fenced or cut by a plough. Kit Carson's parents headed west from Virginia to settle in Missouri; Granville Stuart's parents' destination was Illinois. In both cases, the sons kept going, although not to farm.

The iconic quarter-section, which seemed to so many the solution to all their difficulties, was itself problematic. It was too much for a single family whose aim was subsistence farming, and not enough to make the production of cash crops with hired help worth the effort or expense. And cash crops were anyway worthless unless there was a way of getting them to market. Settlers arrived with basic tools and often with inappropriate old country attitudes to farming. That was probably also a factor in pushing them west. In Kansas, of those who settled between 1854 and 1860, only 35 per cent remained after five years. Quarter-sections were worthless if they were without sufficient water. A settler who failed to secure a water source would very soon be in serious trouble. A year or two of drought could bring ruin; overuse could result in rivers running dry.

The Scots who settled the prairie territories were in the company of mainly other northern Europeans – German and Scandinavian names, as well as English, Welsh and Irish, are those that appear most in the accounts. Many of them shared the same background of sub-sistence farming, pressure on the land, eviction, and agricultural improvement reducing the demand for labour. These were the people who populated the vast areas that were at first deemed to be impossible to cultivate. Scots were well used to coaxing crops out of unpromising soil.

Their task was aided by a fellow Scot, James Oliver, who left his home town of Newcastleton, Roxburghshire, in 1835 to go first to New York, then to Indiana. At South Bend he started an iron-foundry business. One of its main products was a new type of plough, used on thousands of virgin acres. At the height of his business he had 2,000 employees producing 20,000 ploughs a year. The success of farming in the West depended not only on the people who laboured to raise crops, but also on those who supplied the equipment and materials necessary, and there were plenty of Scots who brought entre-preneurial rather than agricultural skills to bear on the enterprise.

Trees were scarce in the Great Plains, and often the first home of the prairie homesteader was a dirt-floored sod house. The Gilchrist family from Ayrshire, William and Janet and their 10 children, lived in a sod house when they first settled in Kansas. Crossing Nebraska in 1879, Robert Louis Stevenson reflected on what it was like to make a home in 'a quarter of the universe laid bare in all its gauntness'. He described a 'town' along the route, 'a dozen wooden houses ... planted along the railway lines', each house isolated and apart. Yet having painted a dispiriting picture, he commented that 'perhaps with sunflowers and cicadae, summer and winter, cattle, wife and family, the settler may create a full and varied existence'.

The work of the pioneer homesteader on the plains was incessant, for men, women and children, as it was for those who settled in the forested territories to the east. It was often many years before there was anything like a community, with a school, a church, a store, and families had to be self-reliant. Neighbours helped each other out, but the nearest neighbour could be many miles away. They would collaborate over harvesting and threshing, and the ranchers got together for round-ups. Scots gained a reputation for skill with agricultural machinery. In the township of Scotland, South Dakota, Scottish farmers co-operated to purchase and operate a threshing machine, which served the community and was a useful source of income.

The sod-busters were looked down on by the free-spirited cattlemen, who despised the farmers' way of life and resented their taking up land claims that intruded on their range. The farmer ploughing on foot with oxen or mules, scraping a living, having to support a family – although the family provided labour – and often burdened by debt, could not compete with the ranchers who seemed to command the landscape, moving with ease on their horses over a vast terrain. It is a comparison that features over and over again in Westerns, with Scottish names appearing in both guises. John Clay's portrait of homesteaders is disparaging, with only grudging acknowledgement of their role:

> You can fight armies or disease or trespass, but the settler never. He advances slowly, surely, silently, like a great motor truck, pushing everything before him. He is cringing in distress, autocratic in prosperity, and yet he is a builder, a great Western asset, peopling a childless land, planting schools by the side of cattle corals, preaching in their practical way the new salvation that is coming to the arid West.

In contrast, the efforts of Wyoming's pioneering cattlemen remained 'a luminous light over the valley and divide'.

In the early 1870s, the time when the potential of investment in the American West was beginning to attract serious Scottish attention, the son of a Banffshire crofter came up with a plan not to buy a cattle ranch but to establish a Scottish colony in Kansas. George Grant had made money from selling crepe to a nation in mourning at the death of Prince Albert. He decided to put the money into American land. He bought over 30,000 acres of railroad land near Hays City, and set about recruiting Scots and others to settle a township he called Victoria.

He wanted people with capital and skills, but he also aimed his promotional literature at crofters and tenant farmers. There was some response, but not enough to attract sufficient numbers to give the project the solid beginnings it needed. Grant had high ambitions, but he died in 1878, before he was able to put most of them into effect, and his scheme petered out. Discouraged by drought and a plague of grasshoppers, many of Grant's Scottish settlers drifted away. But one lasting consequence remained: Grant was responsible for introducing Aberdeen Angus cattle into Kansas.

It was only after the Civil War that the prairie sod-buster became a key feature of western settlement, and it wasn't until the end of the century that old methods of subsistence farming began to give way to techniques of dry farming on what would become a vast scale. It would have been beyond the imagination of the 1870s homesteader to envisage the rolling acres of grain that began to cover Kansas, Nebraska and the Dakotas, punctuated by grain elevators and sliced by railroad tracks, both a vital part of the process of getting the wheat to market.

On the west coast the environment was very different. There, many Scots were prominent in agriculture and horticulture. Several left a lasting mark on the California landscape. When Robert Louis Stevenson visited California's Napa Valley in 1880, he was keen to inspect its vineyards. 'I was interested in Californian wine,' he wrote. 'Indeed, I am interested in all wines, and have been all my life.' His interest in wine is not surprising – the Scots had for centuries been keen importers of claret. What was less expected was to find that one of the vineyards he visited was established by a Scot, Mr M'Ekron from Greenock: 'we exchanged a word or two of Scots, which pleased me more than you would fancy'. M'Ekron had carved out from a wooded slope space to plant his vines – 'there they lie basking in sun and silence' – and to make a modest start at wine-making:

> Mr M'Ekron's is a bachelor establishment; a little bit of a wooden house, a small cellar hard by in the hillside, and a patch of vines planted and tended single-handed by himself. He had but recently begun; his vines were young, his business young also; but I thought he had the look of a man who succeeds.

Next to M'Ekron were the much larger vineyards belonging to the Schrams, where Stevenson was welcomed with 'serious gusto' and an invitation to taste a great variety of wines, which he responded to with evident pleasure: 'the stirring sunlight, and the growing vines, and the vats and bottles in the cavern, made a pleasant music for the mind'.

California was appealing territory for Scottish fruit growers. Alexander Henry, who was born in Leith, abandoned a career in the merchant navy when in 1867 he left his ship to make a new start in California. He acquired land at Anaheim, south of Los Angeles, where he at first set up a winery. When his vines were attacked by blight, he switched to growing oranges and walnuts, and did well. He called his fruit farm Caledonia Grove. John Muir, too, made a success of a fruit farm in California, but his first employment in the Sierras was as a herder of sheep. He had no shepherding experience, but Scottish shepherds and their dogs would become kenspeckle in the West, and it may have been assumed even in the 1870s that caring for sheep was something that all Scots could turn their hands to.

In 1865 Robert Taylor had left Hawick in the Scottish Borders and arrived finally in Wyoming, via Pennsylvania and California. Starting out with a sheep-shearing job, he acquired his own small flock and went on to success as sheep rancher and politician: he was elected to the Wyoming state legislature. He spearheaded what was in effect an invasion of Scottish sheepmen. Although sheep had played an important part in Scottish agriculture for hundreds of years, the rapid increase in numbers in the late 18th century brought radical change to traditional Highland and island subsistence farming and destruction to many communities. The consequences had a widespread impact on North America, as shiploads of displaced Scots were impelled westward. When in the second half of the 19th century thousands of Highland acres were given over to grouse and deer, it was the gamekeeper rather than the shepherd who was in demand. In addition, parts of the Highlands were being overgrazed, and disease was an increasing problem.

While this was happening, ranchers in the western United States' mountain territories were recognising the potential of sheep. They were less labour-intensive than cattle – 3,000 sheep could be cared for by one shepherd and two dogs – and yielded more profit. Some cattle ranchers gave up their cows for sheep. While the sheep population in the Scottish Highlands declined, numbers in the West were growing rapidly; by the 1880s there were four million sheep just in New Mexico. Those who stuck with cattle were hostile. They considered grasslands their exclusive preserve and sheep inferior beasts that close-cropped the grass and made it useless for cattle and horses.

As sheep numbers grew, so did the number of Scottish shepherds, many of whom, like Robert Taylor, began as hired help before acquiring flocks of their own. Taylor became one of the biggest sheep ranchers in Wyoming and Nebraska. By 1913 he was owner of 75,000 acres on which he ran 65,000 sheep as well as cattle and horses. He put a great deal of effort into improving the breed. Another highly successful Scottish sheep rancher was Alan Patterson, who with his Irish partner Patrick Healy had by 1897 built up a flock of 100,000 sheep. The Macfie brothers from the Isle of Bute were running sheep in Wyoming in the early 20th century. W.A. (Scotty) Mackay started his working life in the Clyde shipyard of Denny Brothers, and was also a successful footballer. In 1893 he left the Clyde for New York, and continued west to Wyoming, where after a time repairing locomotives for the Union Pacific Railroad he used his football earnings to start a sheep ranch.

Further west, in Washington, three brothers whose parents were from the Isle of Mull started a sheep ranch in 1882. The success of Archie, Peter and John McGregor was earned through astute understanding and hard work. Across the border in Idaho, Andrew Little from Moffat arrived in Caldwell in 1894, and began working on the sheep ranch of his fellow Scot, Robert Aikman. Gradually, he built up his own herd. In 1901, he returned to Scotland to acquire a wife and persuade seven of his eight brothers to join him in developing what became an enormously successful sheep ranch in the Boise Basin, which was already well populated by Scots. Little became known as the 'Sheep King of Idaho'. Historian Ferenc Szasz describes him as 'the Andrew Carnegie of western life'. Other Scottish sheep ranchers in Idaho included James Laidlaw and Finlay Mackenzie.

There were plenty of Scottish success stories. Robert Burnett from Aberdeenshire ran a large and profitable herd of sheep in California, and Robert Taylor wasn't the only Scot to arrive with nothing but shepherding skills and go on to become a large-scale sheep rancher. William Dunbar from Inverness made a success of sheep ranching in New Mexico's Estancia Valley east of the Rio Grande. In the same area were the McIntosh brothers, William, Donald and John, who arrived in the 1880s and whose name is commemorated by the town of McIntosh. They in turn employed more Scots to herd their flocks, some of whom, it seems, wore the kilt on the job.

David Gowan from Kincardineshire became a homesteader and sheepfarmer almost by accident. In 1877, Gowan was prospecting in the area that is now northern Arizona's Tonto State Park when he was spotted by Apaches. In his attempt to escape he hid in a cavern under a vast natural stone arch. The pursuing Apaches gave up the chase, but Gowan decided to stay put. He claimed the bridge and surrounding area, built a homestead and brought in sheep. He was eventually joined by his nephew David Gowan Goodfellow, who travelled from Scotland with his family, taking the train to Flagstaff followed by a six-day journey south by wagon. Although initially dismayed when they reached the edge of the canyon and saw the steep trail that led down to the homestead, they took over running the farm. With an eye to attracting tourists to the area, David Goodfellow built a lodge for visitors, which still exists.

In spite of impressive examples of success, the experience of most Scottish American sheepmen was much more mundane. They hired out as shepherds, or made a living with relatively small flocks, in unforgiving terrain and in a constant battle with severe winters and dry summers. Ivan Doig's memoir of Montana, *This House of Sky*, gives a flavour of what it was like. Those who homesteaded towards the end of the 19th century tended to have little choice but to take the less hospitable land that remained in the public domain. For the Doig family, and others from Scotland, this meant a location high in the foothills, with the 'cold, storm-making mountains' towering above, 'a slab of lofty country which often would be too cold and dry for their crops, too open to a killing winter for their cattle and sheep':

> It might take a bad winter or a late and rainless spring to bring out this fact, and the valley people did their best to live with calamity whenever it descended. But over time, the altitude and climate added up pitilessly, and even after a generation or so of trying the valley, a settling family might take account and find that the most plentiful things around them were sagebrush and wind.

Or as he put it in *English Creek*, one of several novels that drew on his Montana experience: 'Any place you looked you saw people who had put 20 years into this country and all they had to show for it was a pile of old calendars.'

The Doigs eventually had to give up their homestead, as did many others. Ivan Doig's father worked for several different ranches, spending 'all but a few years of his life riding out after cattle and sheep across the gray sage distances of the Smith River Valley', and Doig himself as a boy and a young man worked with sheep. Peter Doig, his grandfather, spent his first few years in Montana doing 'the jobs on sheep ranches that his son would do a generation later, and which I would do a generation after that, as his son's son – working in the lambing sheds, herding, wrangling in the shearing pens'. Peter Doig 'had all the chance in the world to learn about sheep – and sheep in their gray thousands were the wool-and-meat machines which had made fortunes for the lairds of the Scotland he had arrived from'. There were plenty of Scots around him: 'the burr of their talk could be heard wherever the slow tides of sheep were flowing out onto the grass'.

Peter built a log cabin and filed for his quarter-section, raising sheep, cattle and children, with names that 'began to resound like the roll call of a kilted regiment'. Charles Campbell Doig, Ivan's father, was nine when his father died in an accident. He and his brothers were precipitated into work as hired hands as soon as they were big enough. Their wages kept the homestead going. Charles Doig worked as cowboy and sheep herder, and as a lumberman in Washington. He became an expert horseman. In Ivan's story of his father's life, Scottish names crop up constantly. For a time, Charles worked for Jap Stewart, a one-eyed, hard-drinking Scottish Missourian who was 'a ranchman to the marrow'. A major and threatening landowner in the area was a Helena lawyer called Rankin. The doctor who delivered Ivan was called McKay.

At around the time Charlie Doig was working on Montana ranches, Nellie Ettles Allan from Keith, Banffshire, was getting used to being a farmer's wife in Idaho. As well as the usual domestic chores, she cooked for the hired help and boarders who stayed in the house, raised chickens, and looked after 'bum lambs' – the farm had about 2,000 sheep. She had come to Idaho at the age of 15, worked for an aunt who insisted she scrub the kitchen floor twice a day, and then in a dairy where every morning she was up at four o'clock so she could milk 10 cows, carry water a quarter of a mile as there was no piped water to the dairy, and scrub the milk cans. Sixty years later, she considered that she had had 'a good life ... Much better than I ever had at home'.

The Doigs never made it as big-time sheep ranchers, but neither did they give up on Montana. Their dogged persistence and genuine commitment to a harsh terrain and its demands could be seen as characteristic of their native land. Third-generation Ivan did move west, to Seattle, but retained his intimacy with his Montana upbringing and expressed it in his books, where he also conveys a sense of continuity with the old country.

The Doigs arrived in Montana in the wake of the Great Northern Railroad, and may well have responded to the company's efforts to encourage the settlement it needed to ensure its profits. Scotland was targeted by pamphlets and publicity. A huge boost to the campaign to promote settlement came with the publication of a book by Vermont-born Scottish American Hardy Campbell, *Campbell's Soil Culture Manual.* In it he argued that semi-arid regions, such as the Montana high plateau, could be made productive by a system of scientific soil culture. He had demonstrated, he claimed, that evaporation of 'the soil waters' could be prevented by 'proper cultivation', which would bring 'better crops, better homes, better people, happier children, and a better and more prosperous country'. Small farms were the answer, run by families who would thus be able to improve themselves through hard work and the material rewards it would bring. His ideas found favour in the press. 'Mr Campbell,' wrote a journalist in *The World's Work* magazine, 'without irrigation, can make crops grow on thousands of semi-arid square miles of 'desert' that otherwise would be fruitless and flowerless. In the natural habitat of the cactus, he grows wheat, corn, and vegetables.' It was a gift to the railroad's publicity machine.

James J. Hill, Scottish American dynamo of the Great Northern, was complicit in promoting a vision of comfortable and stable communities. 'Churches and schools will be erected where now bands of cattle and sheep roam; not that cattle and sheep are not all right but farms are better'. Farms suggested families, while cattle ranching invoked an altogether rougher, less communitarian image of free-ranging impermanence. James Hill linked the railways with farms, family life, modest prosperity, rooted security, and progress:

Looking far into the future one may see this region dotted with fine farms, with countless herds of blooded animals grazing, with school houses in every township, with branch lines of railroads, with electric interurban trolley lines running a thousand directions, with telephone systems innumerable, with rural mail routes reaching to every door. It is coming just as sure as the coming of another century. The key has been found and the door to the riches has been unlocked.

Those who responded to this rosy prediction faced a reality of a severe climate, with plenty of snow and hail but little rain in the summer months, and the additional hazard of devastating grasshopper plagues. The end-of-century last phase of the pioneering homesteader was for many a serious disappointment. Homesteading families were no longer the heroic fulfillers of an American dream, independent and courageous, benefiting themselves as they built communities and opened up the frontier, but the rear guard in an unequal struggle against the land and the elements. 'It wasn't long,' writes Jonathan Raban in his book about Montana, *Bad Land* (1996), 'before the society built by the homesteaders came tumbling down about their ears and forced most of them into a farther western exile.' Yet, as the Doig family story expresses, whether they moved on or whether they stayed, their lives retained a heroic quality. The prairie sod-buster and the mountain shepherd were scarcely romantic figures, yet their resilience and tenacity were essential ingredients of the frontier story.

CHAPTER 7

Gold, Silver and the Iron Road

Across the rolling prairies
By steam we're bound to go,
The railroad cars are coming, humming
Through New Mexico.

'The Railroad Cars are Coming'. Traditional,
as sung by Margery Forsythe

ROBERT STUART, son of a Scottish emigrant, left his farm near
Cedar Rapids, Illinois, and with three other men headed for
California. It was 1849. Their destination was the Sacramento
River, where in January 1848 a man called James Marshall, who
worked for John Sutter, picked up something small and yellow
from the river bank. Marshall and Sutter tried to keep their discovery secret, but inevitably word leaked out. The Gold Rush was on.

Robert Stuart reached Sacramento in the autumn of 1849 and
began prospecting for gold, with no great success. After two years
he gave up and returned home, but the following year set off again,
this time with his sons Granville and James. They followed the well-established wagon route from Council Bluffs to the Platte, and on
to Fort Laramie and Fort Hall, and then taking the California trail.
It was 1852, and now the gold fields were filled with activity:

> On all the streams in all the gulches and high up in the Sierras to
> the north, clear to the Oregon line every little camp was crowded
> with miners and gold was being taken out in such profusion as
> almost to lead one to believe that there would be over-production.

Much of the gold acquired was quickly spent. Wherever there were miners, there were those who supplied their needs – provisions, equipment and entertainment. Most of the supplies came via San Francisco, and none of them came cheap. There were plenty of temptations for miners with leisure and funds on their hands. Saloons, brothels and gambling halls were in profusion. Stuart describes the latter, 'magnificently fitted up with plate glass mirrors, brilliant lights shown from chandeliers, and upon a balcony at one end of the hall would be a string band, usually consisting of two violins, and banjo'. The halls were always crowded, with thousand dollar bets not uncommon. 'Some won, some lost, but of course in the long run the dealers were sure winners. The supply of gambling suckers was endless.' Jack Gunn (a name from the north of Scotland) won nearly $4,000 during one night of playing faro in a California mining camp saloon. How long he hung on to it is not recorded. Gambling wasn't confined to the halls: there were also horse races, cock fights and dog fights to bet on. In the larger towns there were dance halls, music halls and theatres. It's not surprising that the fastest way to make money in the gold fields was not by digging and sluicing for gold, but by providing services for those who seemed only too eager to part with what they toiled to obtain.

James Thomson was a baker's apprentice in Aboyne, Aberdeenshire, but left for Canada in 1844. Five years later he, too, joined the stream of hopefuls setting off from Council Bluffs to hunt for gold. He took with him a tent and cooking stove, along with provisions for four months. He accomplished the 2,500 mile journey to Placerville and Nevada City without mishap. In a letter home he wrote: 'No doubt hundreds ... will be disappointed, still there is better chance of success in going there than by embarking in any sort of business with the same amount of capital'. After a spell involved in a Nevada City lumber business, with two others he bought a claim for $1,000, which yielded a reasonable living. He returned to his original trade of baking but continued to prospect for gold.

In the summer of 1853, the elder Stuart went back to Iowa, but the sons remained, moving into the Sierra Nevada for more prospecting. Two years later they were heading north, to the Klamath River in Oregon. James joined troops fighting the Modoc Indians. Granville continued prospecting, and became friendly with the Grant family, who had a log cabin on the Beaverhead. He celebrated Christmas with the Grants, with a meal of buffalo meat, boiled smoked tongue, bread, dried fruit, chokecherry preserve and coffee. Granville had some success in finding gold, but by the summer of 1858 was buying oxen and horses, and fattening them up on mountain grass before re-selling them. James re-joined Granville, and they tried a variety of trades while still looking for gold. They ran a butcher's shop, set up a blacksmith's in Bannock, Montana, opened a store in Virginia City, which had become the centre of another bonanza. When they sold up the butcher's business, Granville Stuart left town with $3,000 in gold dust. He was trailed by three men whom he suspected of intending to rob him, but managed to shake them off.

Gold brought people to Nevada, Colorado, Idaho, Oregon and Montana, and the scenes that Granville Stuart described in California repeated themselves. Many gave up the hope of making an easy fortune, some returned east, others stayed in the west and, like Granville, turned to commercial activities or to farming. But the mining camps attracted predators as well as prospectors and their camp followers, and were breeding grounds of crime. Scottish names crop up frequently in descriptions of violent incidents, on either side of the law. In 1880 the federal census gave the total population of Bodie in the Sierra Nevada, a mining community that in that year reached the height of its success, as 5,373, of which 120 were born in Scotland. There must have been more who were of Scottish descent, and of the 850 born in Ireland a significant number would have been Ulster Scots.

The people of the nearby mining town of Aurora elected as their sheriff N.F. Scott, whose task it was to impose order on an unruly and fluctuating population. As well as robbery and clashes over claims, there were frequent brawls, fuelled by alcohol, which often resulted in serious injury or death. A typical incident involving Scots erupted in August 1864, when the deputy sheriff's arrest of Charles Gillespie for disturbing the peace provoked an outburst that landed half-a-dozen or so drunken brawlers in jail. Miner John E. Campbell, an Ulster Scot, had a reputation for being easily aroused and was frequently involved in spats and altercations. In June 1864 he got into an argument with a man called Parlin, in the Del Monte Exchange saloon. Things quickly got out of hand. The men drew their pistols, but both missed, whereupon Parlin used his gun to batter Campbell on the head. In the course of the ensuing struggle, Parlin fired two shots into Campbell, who died a few hours later. The *Aurora Times* described him as a man of courage, 'warm hearted, generous, outspoken and manly; but, unfortunately, like so many of his countrymen, high-tempered and impulsive to rashness'.

Bodie saw similar incidents. Alex Nixon (a Scottish Border name) was the Irish-born president of the Bodie Miners' Union and in the early hours of 13 June 1878 was drinking in the Shamrock saloon. A quarrel broke out between him and Tom McDonald which resulted in blows and shots being exchanged. Nixon was hit in the side, and died. Although McDonald was arrested and jailed, charges against him were dropped. Another Scot, Thomas Hamilton, survived two gunshot wounds, while Burns Buchanan was involved in at least one shooting incident. Territorial disputes were also frequent.

It was 1860 when gold was discovered in this part of the Sierra Nevada. The town of Aurora was laid out in 1861. At that time, apart from prospectors, there were a few isolated ranchers, and scattered bands of Paiute Indians, who in the early 1860s and sporadically thereafter resisted white incursions. In particular, they regarded as their territory the Owens Valley, good grazing land south of Aurora and Bodie. A military post was established there, but efforts were made to avoid a war with the Paiutes and a reservation was organised. However, as gold attracted more and more whites into the area the Paiutes felt increasingly threatened, and inevitably

The Cheyenne Club, Cheyenne, Wyoming, 1880s.
Membership included many Scottish ranchers.

University of Wyoming Library.

Cheyenne, Wyoming, 1882.
A centre for cattle ranching where Scots were prominent.

University of Wyoming Library.

Campaign against the Sioux, Montana, 1876. One of the commanders was
Scottish American General George Crook. It is remembered particularly for
the Battle of the Little Bighorn, in which General George Armstrong Custer,
also of partly Scots descent, lost his life.

Library of Congress.

Mt Rainier, Washington State, an area explored and settled by Scots.
The mountain, over 14,000 ft high, was climbed by John Muir in 1888.

James Christie from Morayshire, who in 1889 led an expedition exploring the Olympic area in the northwest tip of Washington State.

John Muir. Muir, born 1838 in Dunbar, emigrated to Wisconsin as a young boy. He grew up to initiate the American conservation movement.

Library of Congress.

Miners on their way through the Rocky Mountains to new diggings, 1875.
Many Scots joined the search for gold, silver and copper.

Frenzeny & Tavernier, Library of Congress.

Crossing the plains, from the Pioneers' Ten Commandments, 1849.
Kurz & Allison's Art Studio, Chicago, c.1887. Library of Congress.

At work in a gold mine in Eagle River Canyon, Colorado, c.1905.

H. C. White Co, Library of Congress.

Sluicing and panning for gold in California, the methods used by
independent prospectors such as Granville and James Stuart in the 1850s.

Currier & Ives, Library of Congress.

American Progress by George A. Crofutt, c.1873.
An allegorical female figure as a symbol of pioneers following the westward moving frontier.

Branding on the XIT ranch, c.1904, one of many Scottish-owned ranches in Texas.
Library of Congress.

Ploughing on the prairie beyond the Mississippi by Theodore R. Davis, 1868.
Many Scots were among those who homesteaded west of the Mississippi
after the Civil War.

Library of Congress.

Autumn round-up on a Montana ranch. A large number of Montana
and Wyoming ranches were Scottish owned.

Library of Congress.

Cowboys herding cattle on the XIT ranch, Texas, 1903.
W.D. Harper, Library of Congress.

Bronco-busting on the XIT ranch, Texas.
Library of Congress.

attacked. Prospectors William McDonald and the Ayres brothers were camped on Big Pine Creek, a tributary of the Owens River, when the Paiute appeared at dusk. McDonald, wounded by four arrows, was tracked down and stoned to death by his attackers. Sheriff Scott, Harrison Morrison and Sergeant Christopher Gillespie of the 2nd Cavalry, California Volunteers, were among those killed when bands of Paiute united to mount an assault on local ranchers and prospectors. The captain of Aurora's defenders was Charles Anderson.

The frontier was a dangerous place, but much of the violence was self-generated, the result of intensely competitive living, high expectations that were often disappointed, easy access to weapons and liquor, and a dearth of women and domestic comforts. All mining camps were unstable, but Bodie became notorious, and the local press was concerned about the 'bad men of Bodie' image. Reporting a killing in December 1878, the *Bodie Standard* commented:

> There is some irresistible power in Bodie which impels us to cut and shoot each other to pieces... The clashing of revolvers up and down Main Street can be constantly heard, and it sounds as if we were enjoying a perpetual Chinese Fourth of July. Scarcely a man in town wears a suit of clothes but has more or less holes in it ... everybody must fight who comes to Bodie.

Three years later the *Daily Free Press* was more tongue-in-cheek:

> Times are dull, money scarce and the weather miserable. Under such a condition of affairs there must be some inexpensive recreation provided for the people. Six-shooters are of no account unless they can be used, and coffins will warp and be unfit for occupancy if allowed to stand a great while in an undertaker's room. In India mothers throw their children into the river when the number is too large, and nothing is said about it, but when Bodie is over-crowded and a man is put out of the way to make room for a new arrival, a great howl goes up and we are called a 'hard crowd'.

Sport was another outlet for frustration, and wrestling in particular was popular. Prominent among participants were miners Rod McInnis and Dan McMillan. McInnis was particularly impressive. According to the *Bodie Standard*, he was of muscular build, remarkably agile, and highly skilled. On one occasion when the referee disallowed a clear McInnis victory, spectators took matters into their own hands. In the words of the *Daily Free Press*, 'the immense crowd made a rush for the sidewalk, carrying the doors along with it. Lights were put out, chairs thrown about, windows and lamps broken.'

Although attempts were made to curb the lawlessness, there was little chance in the early days of these communities of introducing any kind of civic infrastructure. Families were rare, schools and churches alien concepts. Alexander McClure was travelling in Colorado and Montana in 1867 and passed through a number of mining camps. He remarked that miners were disinclined to 'cramp themselves' with religion:

> Such a thing as a sermon I have neither heard nor heard of since I have been in Union City. Occasionally a stray shepherd comes along to look after his stray sheep wandering through the mountains, but as a rule the shepherd gets lost among the sheep, seems to prefer the glittering nuggets of gold from the gulches and mines to the promised glittering stars in his future crown for the salvation of souls.

Bonanzas came and went, and a rootless population followed each new find. Granville Stuart's wanderings in the 1850s are typical. In later decades, each new mining town replicated the disorder of the one before. Here is the town of Murray, Idaho, clearly named for a Scot, described by a journalist in the October 1884 issue of *Century Magazine*.

> It is composed of a hideous half-mile-long street of huts, shanties, and tents, with three or four cross-streets that run against the steep slopes after a few rods of progress... A more unattractive

place than Murray I have seldom seen. The trees have been cleared away, leaving a bare gulch into which the sun pours for sixteen hours a day with a fervour which seems to be designed by nature to make up for the coolness of the short July nights, when fires are needed. Stumps and half-charred logs encumber the streets, and serve as seats for the inhabitants... Every second building is a drinking saloon...

Men with nothing to do hung about the saloons and swore 'in all styles of profanity known to a miners' vocabulary'. But although there were large numbers without employment, gold was being shipped out daily by Well's Fargo, and there were constant new strikes.

In the early 1870s gold prospectors were beginning to penetrate Dakota's Black Hills. One of them was James 'Scotty' Philip from Morayshire, who arrived in 1874, the year when gold was found, near the present day town of Custer. The Black Hills, sacred to the Sioux, were officially protected from white incursion. In fact, George Armstrong Custer and his troops, whose job it was to keep prospectors out, made only half-hearted efforts to turn back the ensuing flood. When the Sioux turned down an offer on the part of government negotiators to purchase the Black Hills, the army gave up any pretence of restriction. Miners swarmed into South Dakota. The train of events that led to George Crook being called north and to Custer's death at the Little Big Horn had begun. Scotty Philip abandoned his search for gold in 1877, and like Granville Stuart turned to ranching. He would eventually make his mark by conserving one of the last surviving buffalo herds.

Alex Mackay, born in Perth, struck it lucky in Arizona. He arrived in the US after the Civil War, trying his hand at sheep farming in California before making his way east. North of Tucson, he found gold, on Christmas Day 1878. He named his mine after the day of discovery, and a week later discovered another, which he named the New Year mine. He built the first house of what became the town of Oracle. Five years later he added the Peer and Peerless mines to his collection. Further north, in Nevada, discovery of gold and silver in a ravine above the Carson Valley had in 1859 generated first a massive stampede to exploit the Comstock Lode, and then the formation of the Comstock Company. Alex Mackay sold his claims to the company for $30,000 and spent his latter years in Tucson. In 1926, when he was in his 80s, he was arrested and jailed for the possession of bootleg whisky, but received a presidential pardon in recognition of his contribution to the development of Arizona.

Another Comstock Mackay, John, became known as the 'Bonanza King' through his mining activities. John Mackay had been a shipwright back east before heading for California in 1851. At first, Mackay was prospecting, before working on contract, digging shafts and inserting timber props. Then, with three others, he was able to put money into the Comstock Lode. The four of them became, in the words of J.C. Furnas, 'the plutocratic kings of silver-mad Nevada'. Mackay, transformed into a successful businessman, travelled in a lavish private car on the Virginia and Truckee Railroad, which linked the Nevada mining camps with the Central Pacific Railroad.

The Comstock Lode eventually yielded $300,000,000, of which another beneficiary was Eilley Orrum, who emigrated from Scotland as a Mormon convert. After two failed marriages and several years in Salt Lake City she moved on to the Carson Valley, where she maintained herself by taking in miners' laundry and providing board and lodging. One miner paid his rent with a 10-foot claim, unaware that it was rich in silver. When Eilley married Sandy Bowers, holder of the next-door claim, it proved to be a lucrative partnership. With their joint claim bringing in $50,000 a year, Mrs Bowers was able to build a splendid mansion and travel to Europe, where she was disappointed that her 'Queen of the Comstock' moniker did not open the door to an audience with Queen Victoria. Eventually the claim was worked out and, by this time a widow, Eilley Bowers spent her latter years as a fortune teller in California, an occupation which suggests that her own luck did not hold.

There was more gold to be discovered. Near Cripple Creek in Colorado the first signs of what would be described as the world's biggest gold producing location were found in October 1890, and six years later gold was discovered in Alaska. When the Cripple Creek miners went on strike in 1894, one of their leaders was John Calderwood from Glasgow. Another Glaswegian, John Stewart MacArthur, in 1889 introduced to Colorado mines the cyanide process of extracting gold from mine waste. The process was widely adopted, and more than doubled the world's annual output of gold.

One of many fictional accounts of mining communities is found in *Canyon Passage* by Ernest Haycox (1945), which locates its action in the real town of Jacksonville, on the border between Oregon and California. His central character is Logan Stuart, who runs a freight business between Jacksonville and Portland, 'a man of loose and rough and durable parts, like a machine intended for hard usage'. There are several other Scottish names: Portland businessman Henry McLane, Jacksonville prospector Mack McIver, bankers Crawford & Co, poker-playing merchant Neil Howison. As Stuart enters Jacksonville with his mule train he passes the brush lean-tos, tents and log cabins of the miners along the creek, before coming into the main street. It is a settlement of around sixty houses 'built of logs and riven cedar stakes, all scattered along the creek and up the side of the surrounding hills'. The men strolling in the streets are 'stained by the yellow-green clay of the diggings'. Haycox weaves through his plot of murder and revenge a vivid picture of a rough-edged community struggling to begin the transition to a civilised town.

Gold, silver and then copper were the main mineral attractions in the West, but after the Civil War, with westward advancement of the railroads, coal became increasingly important. Coal fields opened up in Kansas, Oklahoma, Wyoming, Colorado, Utah, California and Washington. Scottish expertise in mining was widely recognised, and the recruitment of mine managers, as well as miners, directly from Scotland was common. Scots were aware of US job opportunities in the coal mines, and responded to the appeal of much higher wages (though conditions were often worse than at home). Cheap transatlantic fares were offered. It was worthwhile to work temporarily in America, with the aim of returning to Scotland well set up. But of course, many Scots remained in the US. John Wallace was one of them: born in Coatbridge in the Lanarkshire coalfield and trained as an engineer, he became manager of a mine in Ohio before opening his own mine. He moved west to South Dakota, where he became owner of a retail coal company.

Scots provided manpower for mining all over the US; they also provided money. Although mining didn't generate the same excitement as cattle, Scottish investment in the extractive industries was considerable, beginning cautiously in the 1870s and increasing in the following decade. But it was not a great success. In 1881, for example, the Scottish Pacific Coast Mining Company was set up, and bought from Charles Sutherland claims in Sierra County, California, for $400,000. The company easily attracted investment from Scots. But it transpired that the claims were virtually worthless and the company had to go into liquidation.

Colorado mining also attracted Scottish investment, but again without results. Scots, particularly in Glasgow, were keen to put their money into mining infrastructure and technology. Historian W. Turrentine Jackson commented: 'Glasgow solicitors and accountants encountered little difficulty in locating ironmakers, wine merchants, and ship builders who were willing to risk a few thousand pounds in the search for gold and silver, to introduce a new technological process, or even to underwrite or refinance a declining mine.' Glasgow shipbuilder Leonard Low and publishers Walter and Robert Blackie were among those who put funds into hydraulic mining operations on the Feather River in California. The technology required substantial investment and the process was expensive to run, but the mines did not produce enough gold to make it worthwhile.

The success story, although only after travelling a very rocky road, was the Arizona Copper Company, sponsored by the Scottish American Mortgage Company and registered in 1882. It was at once oversubscribed by an eager public. Copper mining had been underway in New Mexico and Arizona since the 1860s, but there were problems with shipping out and smelting the ore. When the Southern Pacific Railroad reached Lordsburg, it became more feasible to transport the copper ore the 75 miles from the mines to be loaded onto trains that connected with ports on the Gulf of Mexico. In addition, smelting works had been established at Clifton on the San Francisco River, which the Scottish company also acquired. At first they used locally produced charcoal, and then coke brought from Lordsburg. It was a major operation, employing around 25,000 men, many of them Mexicans and Chinese. The focus of the operation was Graham County.

A larger smelter was built and in 1883 a narrow-gauge railway line was completed, from Lordsburg to Clifton. In late 1882 J. Duncan Smith arrived from Scotland to inspect the progress of a number of Scottish companies. His report was not encouraging and shareholders began to get worried. More inspections followed. Colin Mackenzie, one of the Edinburgh directors, made a visit and returned to Scotland with more favourable news: a smelter had been constructed and a new and rich deposit of ore had been located. A period of some confusion followed, which illustrated the difficulty of getting reliable information from an operation 5,000 miles away from the main source of investment. A crisis of confidence resulted in the resignation of members of the board, including the chairman, and a reconfiguration of the company, but the problems continued, not helped by a largely hostile press. Eventually, the Arizona Copper Company was dissolved and a new company with the same name was registered in 1884.

While in Scotland directors and shareholders struggled to sort out a messy situation, in Arizona work at the mines continued. An inspection at the end of 1884 confirmed that the mines around Clifton were indeed rich in copper ore. The company owned around 40 claims, as well as an increasingly extensive smelting operation and a railway network that connected the mines and smelters, and linked with the completed line to Lordsburg. According to Turrentine Jackson, 'No enterprise in the American West for the production of copper bullion had been so well organised and equipped.' Three of the furnaces had been constructed by Messrs Fraser and Chalmers of Chicago, and two by the equally Scottish-sounding firm of Messrs Rankin, Brayton, and Company of San Francisco.

The Arizona Copper Company's problems were not at an end, however. By the end of 1884, the price of copper was in decline. Although prices recovered, the up-and-down pattern continued. In spite of the many setbacks, including a flood in 1891 which destroyed a railroad bridge across the San Francisco River, the company's Scottish backers stuck to their guns. In 1895 a new general super-intendent of the works was appointed, James Colquhoun, who made a number of technological improvements. He commented:

> Our mining has kept pace with the general forward movement of our metallurgical work, and as a result we are now extracting ore from timbered slopes for a price which in former years would have been deemed impossible. While doing this work, the devel-opment of the mines has been so little neglected that the company has more ore in sight than its present plant can do justice to.

This coincided with an increased demand for copper, caused in part by the need for copper wire as electrical communication expanded. A new era of profitability was entered, which continued for more than two decades, in spite of major flood damage in 1905 and a serious strike in 1915.

In 1921, the Scots sold all the holdings of the Arizona Copper Company to the American corporation of Phelps Dodge. Some of the shareholders opposed the deal, especially when they discovered that their own profit was much less than expected. James Colquhoun recorded their response: 'The blow fell like the news of a second Flodden,' he wrote, and he described the stormy shareholders' meeting, at which the final terms of the sale were announced, as being like clan warfare, 'devoid of all the charms' of YMCA meetings:

The only portion of the Chairman's able speech which attracted appreciation was the announcement that 15 minutes would be allowed for refreshments. The crowd at once proceeded to the nearest bars, and when fortified with the wine of the country, they again drew up in line to meet the shock of battle.

It might almost have been a mining-camp brawl.

Turrentine Jackson lists 37 Western American mining enterprises registered in Scotland between 1872 and 1913. Unlike investment in cattle ranching, where Edinburgh and Dundee dominated, the Scottish headquarters were most often in Glasgow. The mines themselves were located in California, Utah, Arizona, Colorado, Idaho, Montana, South Dakota and Missouri. Where there was Scottish money, there were likely to be Scots. There were certainly frequent visitations from representatives of Scottish companies. Among them were Glasgow coal merchants James Nimmo and George A. Mitchell who were sent to Montana on behalf of a syndicate interested in the Diamond Hill gold mines near Townsend. They worked to utilise modern technology, building a dam and power plant to provide electricity. But they couldn't generate sufficient power, and after struggling for 10 years to make a go of the Diamond Hill mines they were forced to abandon the project. At least £60,000 of Scottish investment was lost.

Other Glasgow ventures included a syndicate which embarked on fruitless mining efforts in Arizona. A Glasgow-based company, instigated by John E. Watson, purchased the Highland Chief Mining Company, operating near Deadwood, South Dakota, only to find the mine was worthless. But these failures did not seem to discourage Scottish interest. Whether Glaswegians were particularly susceptible is hard to say, but they continued to pour money into exploring for gold in the American West. In some cases, they were people with just a small amount of spare cash – an ironmonger, a warehouseman, a teacher, a printer. Turrentine Jackson cites a Glasgow student who purchased two shares. Company after company got nowhere.

In 1896 the ambitious Glasgow and Western Exploration Company was set up, under the sponsorship of J & P Coats, the Paisley thread manufacturers, who had been operating a spinning mill in Rhode Island for several decades. They purchased mines near Milford, Utah, at Cherry Creek, Nevada and Ouray, Colorado. A considerable amount of money and effort went into machinery and equipment, to no avail. Although efforts continued until 1921, they yielded nothing. About £230,000 of Scottish funds, from 'an unsuspecting Scottish public, usually misguided by a Scottish promoter who hoped to share profits with an American vendor', disappeared.

There was, however, an occasional tale of striking success, which of course encouraged continued interest. The Jumper Gold Syndicate was sponsored in 1896 by three Glaswegians, Thomas Lawson, a jeweller, James Ferguson, a butcher and coalmaster George Mitchell. They purchased several mines in Tuolumne County, California, among which the Jumper proved particularly rewarding. It was, according to a report by Californian officials, 'one of the best worked and best managed mines in the state'. It remained productive for 10 years. But the Scots went on to purchase more mines, and much of the Jumper's profits went into extending and modernising the new acquisitions, but with little result: 'a significant percentage of the profits from the Jumper were left behind in Tuolumne County rather than going home to Glasgow'.

In the early 1850s, Scot Laurence Oliphant was travelling in Wisconsin and Minnesota. He took part in an expedition by canoe, following one of the routes planned for a railroad to the Pacific. The railroad was seen as the key to western expansion, and according to Oliphant its progress west was 'the enterprise which lies nearest the heart of every Minnesotian'. From Chicago to the Pacific coast was nearly 2,000 miles, and there was fierce debate as to the merits of rival routes: the railroads would bring economic benefits to the territories affected. One proposal was for a route from St Louis following the Kansas River and through Colorado.

Missourians were keen on this, and keen also to extend their own territorial influence. One of them, nominated in 1853 as delegate to Congress, was Ulster Scot Abelard Guthrie. A rival route would take the railroad from Chicago and up the valley of the Platte, while there were also those who advocated a southern route. The chairman of the Committee on Territories was Scottish American Stephen Douglas – 'the little steam engine in britches', as he was described by his friends. He had the highly politically sensitive task of sorting out the future territories of Kansas and Nebraska and resolving the associated matter of the railroads. He proposed government support for three transcontinental lines.

But the Senate's Pacific Railroad Committee took fright at the cost, and proposed a single route, thus unleashing a further round of intense debate and lobbying. In 1862 Congress passed a bill authorising the Central Pacific and Union Pacific Railroads. Because of the Civil War, the necessary funds, including Scottish money, came slowly, but survey crews were nevertheless soon at work. Among the Scots involved was Arthur N. Ferguson, with the Union Pacific crew. By 1866 most of the line was mapped out, following the Platte through Nebraska and then the South Platte, alongside Lodgepole Creek and across to the Rockies via Cheyenne and Laramie, then through the Wasatch Mountains to the Great Salt Lake. Among the many problems they encountered were Indian attacks. Ferguson helped to fight off one dawn raid trouserless and without his boots.

Construction began in 1863. On 10 May 1869, the Union Pacific from the east and the Central Pacific from California met at Promontory Point in Utah. (The junction was later shifted south, and this historic meeting place no longer exists: the rails were removed during the Second World War.) The impact of this joining of east and west was enormous, and celebrations were nationwide. Cannon were discharged in Chicago, Boston, Sacramento, New York, Pittsburgh, Cleveland, Milwaukee and San Francisco, where there were three days of flags and parades. 'Everywhere,' write railroad historians Lucius Beebe and Charles Clegg, 'fire bells tolled, anvils were smitten, prayers of thanksgiving were offered in holy places and glasses were raised and smashed in more profane resorts.'

Following the laying of track by the Union Pacific as it made its way through Kansas was Alexander Gardner, a Paisley-born photographer hired by the railroad to record its progress. Gardner had photographed the Civil War, working with Matthew Brady, having learned his trade when he was a reporter for a Glasgow newspaper. His task now was to capture not only trains, bridges and the work of construction, but the country the railroad traversed, the Native Americans who occupied it, and the towns that sprang up along the way. Travelling in a wagon which doubled as a dark-room, Gardner produced an impressive and valuable collection of images. The most iconic, depicting a construction gang laying rails with a locomotive looming immediately behind them, was given the resounding title, borrowed from Bishop Berkeley's 'On the Prospect of Planting Arts and Learning in America': 'Westward the Course of Empire Takes its Way'.

In 1873 Isabella Bird ascended the Sierras by train, and evoked in a letter to her sister Henrietta an image of locomotives which Western movies would later make familiar to millions:

> The great gaudy engines ... with their respective tenders loaded with logs of wood, the engines with great, solitary, reflecting lamps in front above the cow guards, a quantity of polished brass-work, comfortable glass houses, and well-stuffed seats for the engine-drivers. The engines and tenders were succeeded by a baggage car, the latter loaded with bullion and valuable parcels...

Another 1870s Scottish traveller on American trains was Robert Louis Stevenson, who, despite an acutely difficult and uncomfortable journey, memorably captured the symbolic and historic resonance of the railroad:

> When I think how the railroad has been pushed through this

unwatered wilderness and haunt of savage tribes, and now will bear an Emigrant for some 12 pounds from the Atlantic to the Golden Gates; how at each stage of the construction, roaring, impromptu cities, full of gold and lust and death, sprang up, and then died away again, and are now but wayside stations in the desert; how in these uncouth places, pig-tailed Chinese pirates worked side by side with border ruffians and broken men from Europe, talking together in a mixed dialect, mostly oaths, gambling, drinking, quarrelling and murdering like wolves; how the plumed, hereditary lord of all America, heard, in this last fastness, the scream of the 'bad medicine waggon', charioting his foes; and then when I go to remember that all this epical turmoil was conducted by gentlemen in frock coats and with a view to nothing more extraordinary than a fortune and subsequent visit to Paris, it seems to me, I own, as if this railway were the one typical achievement of the age in which we live, as if it brought together into one plot all the ends of the world and all the degrees of social rank, and offered to some great writer the busiest, the most extended and the most varied subject for an enduring literary world.

Stevenson's journey on an emigrant train brought him for the first time to the American West, yet he was able to encapsulate in a few sentences an extraordinary breadth of experience.

The Scottish involvement in American railroad history was considerable, in large and small ways. The impact of railroad expansion on Scottish lives affected both sides of the Atlantic. Scots joined the stream of emigrants who were now able to travel, if not in comfort at least speedily (compared with covered wagon) to the Far West. Some responded to the intensive recruitment in Scotland of emigrants to settle railroad lands and build up populations that would sustain railroad traffic. Some of those Scots would work on or for the railroads. John Guthrie, who emigrated from Scotland in the early 1800s, was a director of the Atcheson, Topeka and Santa Fe Railroad, and gave his name to Guthrie, Oklahoma. Alexander Mitchell from Aberdeenshire joined the Wisconsin

Insurance Company at the age of 22, and went on to become a banker and railroad builder, helping to expand the Milwaukee and St Paul Railroad. James Duncan Wallace was born in Edinburgh and worked in railway workshops in Glasgow and Dundee before leaving for Illinois in 1871. He moved from Illinois to Missouri to Kansas, where at Topeka he was employed in the workshops of the Santa Fe Railroad. Later he and his wife acquired a farm near Topeka, which he ran successfully while continuing his railroad work. In 1896 Peter Ross commented: 'There is not a railway machine shop in America, or iron shipbuilding establishment, where Scotch mechanics may not be found.'

Large amounts of Scottish money were invested. With the completion of the transcontinental link, branch lines sprouted in all directions. They served communities, ports, mining and industrial operations, and ranching and agricultural centres. Scots were involved in both railway development and the operations that the railway served. Oregon attracted a lot of attention, and several Scottish companies were involved there. A key figure was William Mackenzie from Dumfriesshire, son of a Free Church minister, who became secretary of the Oregon and Washington Trust Investment Company, which lent money to buy land and build homes and barns. Mackenzie replaced William Reid who, sent out to Oregon by the company in 1873, decided to stay. It was the start of a notable career for Mackenzie, as he became involved with several companies operating in Oregon.

One of them was the Oregonian Railway Company, registered in Scotland in 1880, with people in the Dundee area, including the Earl of Airlie, investing over £300,000. The plan was to develop railroads in Oregon and Washington, linking with railroads outwith these territories and with transportation by road and water. It was a highly ambitious scheme to create, in Turrentine Jackson's words, a 'transportation empire in the Northwest if fate and finances proved favourable'. Neither turned out to be the case, in spite of William Reid, the company's Scottish representative in

Oregon, sending encouraging reports. After struggling to prevail against mounting practical, financial and legal difficulties, the company eventually went into liquidation. Mackenzie commented on the debacle, identifying Reid as chief culprit:

> This is the man who brought to our unfortunate town that sad misadventure the Oregonian Railway, which cost our citizens something like a quarter of a million sterling and years of weary suspense and fierce and futile battle.

But it wasn't just Scottish money that went into American railroads, and in many cases never came out again. There were Scots on the ground, planning, engineering and constructing new lines. One of them was David Moffatt, who built the Denver and Salt Lake Railroad with the profit from mining. The line had got only as far as Craig, Colorado, much less than half way, when his money ran out, but the city of Denver provided more cash through a bond issue, and Moffatt forged on. The Moffatt tunnel through the Rockies is named for him. Moffatt was described by historian David Lavender as 'a dull, patient, acquisitive man', which certainly fits a Scottish stereotype, but he also enjoyed playing poker which is perhaps less compatible.

Another important railroad building Scot was John Murray Forbes, who created through the amalgamation of smaller lines the Chicago, Burlington & Quincy Railroad, one of the main arteries carrying emigrants west across the Great Plains. He was director of the company for over 40 years, and had a reputation as a man who quietly and doggedly got on with the job in hand. But the two most influential Scots in the history of American railroads were John Stewart Kennedy and James Jerome Hill. Kennedy was from Blantyre in Lanarkshire and first spent time in the US from 1850 to 1852, as the representative of an iron and coal firm. Five years later he was back, and started an American career in banking and investment. Railroads attracted his interest. He established the firm of Jessup, Kennedy and Company in Chicago to sell railway supplies: by 1868 he was a wealthy man. In New York he started the banking firm of J.S. Kennedy and Company, and financed a number of railway ventures. One of them was the purchase of the St Paul and Pacific line, which under the guidance of his friend James J. Hill was reborn as the St Paul, Minneapolis and Manitoba Railway, seen as a vital commercial link: 'it brings an empire to our very door,' announced the St Paul *Daily Globe*.

James Hill was born in Ontario, into a family of Scottish and Irish origins. He was brought up on traditional Scottish music, the poetry of Burns and the novels of Scott. In later life, as a successful railroad magnate, he would, according to his biographer Albro Martin, sing the old songs of his childhood 'around campfires in Montana or before the towering fireplaces of exclusive salmon fishing lodges'. His railroad career started in St Paul, where he worked for a steamboat company before setting up his own freight transfer business. This in turn led to his involvement in railroads. With characteristic energy and single-minded determination, he made himself a railroad expert. Trains and track would dominate the rest of his life.

Kennedy and Hill were a powerful team. They were key figures in the syndicate that brought to birth the Canadian Pacific Railway, and so played an important role in populating Canada's western provinces as well as the western states of the US. The Manitoba railroad initially came to an end in Dakota Territory, 80 miles west of the Red River that flowed into Canada. Hill was determined to drive it further. George Stephen, another Scot, whose unflinching determination brought the CPR from the brink of collapse, was clear that 'the Manitoba road ought to extend as rapidly as may be expedient westward south of the boundary line [with Canada], no doubt some day reaching the Pacific Ocean'. The Great Northern, as it became, was competing with the rival Northern Pacific line, which ran further south, taking a route along the Yellowstone River to Montana, which it reached in 1881. The Great Northern followed the Missouri to Great Falls.

Hill closely supervised progress. 'It pays to be where the money is spent,' he had remarked in 1878. In the summer of 1887, a record-breaking 643 miles of track was laid from Minot, Dakota to Helena, Montana. They forged on, backed by George Stephen and another Scot crucial to the success of the Canadian Pacific, Donald Smith. They cut 900 miles through the mountains, bridging rivers and gaping chasms, constructing embankments on steep slopes, and blasting tunnels. They carried on in the face of blizzards and floods. Hill was, according to the project's engineer John Stevens, 'a hard taskmaster... He kept everyone on the jump and not always by suave comments.' On 6 January 1893 the last spike was driven at Scenic, on the west slope of the Cascade Mountains, completing the Great Northern to Seattle. Twelve days later, the first passenger train left St Paul for the west coast.

Later, Hill would gain control of the Northern Pacific and acquire the Burlington road. Andrew Carnegie, the most famous and economically influential of all Scottish Americans, sent him a Christmas note inviting him to dinner: 'Merry Christmas, Colossus! We shall have the two most famous Scots together. J.S. Kennedy, the third Scot is also coming.' Hill had an unshakeable belief in the railroad as 'pathfinder and pioneer', to quote from his own book *Highways of Progress* (1910). 'The railroad has outrun the settler,' he wrote, 'and beckoned him on; has opened up new territory, brought in population, created new industries and new wealth.' It was not just 'a connecting link between communities' but 'a creative energy to bring them into existence'. In 1850, he argued, the Pacific coast was 'almost as unknown as another continent'. By the end of the century, thanks to the railroad, it had joined the rest of the US, and the wilderness had been transformed into 'the home of plenty'. This wasn't the end of the story, but when James Jerome Hill died in 1916 the *New York Times* celebrated him as 'a figure carved in massive proportions out of man's necessity to act heroically upon his hostile environment'. At 2.00 p.m. on the day of his funeral, 31 May, every train on Hill's railroads stopped for five minutes.

CHAPTER 8

Building Communities

Since I never killed a man but what was needin' lead,
They made me sheriff – to keep things straight they said.

'The Dying Desperado', traditional, as sung by Blair Boyd,
cowboy with the Rocking Chair Ranch, Texas

HUGO REID WAS BORN in Cardross, Dunbartonshire, and by the age
of 22 was a merchant in Hermosillo, North Mexico. Two years later
he was trading in Los Angeles, at that time a largely Spanish community. When his business failed he returned to Mexico where he
worked as a teacher, but then was back in California to marry Doña
Victoria, a Native American widow with four children, who had been
brought up in a Spanish mission. The law demanded that, in order to
marry, he had to become a Catholic. He helped his wife pursue her
claim to two ranches in the San Gabriel Valley, successfully overcom-
ing resistance to Native Americans owning land. As well as ranching
and setting up a Pacific trading business with his ship the *Esmeralda*,
which took him as far west as Hawaii, he developed his interest in the
history and customs of Native Californians and became a champion
of their rights. He wrote a number of articles on these topics for the
Los Angeles Star. In 1839 he was elected to Los Angeles city council,
and he later became a justice of the peace.

In one of his *Los Angeles Star* pieces Reid described a Scottish
import to California, the game of shinty, popular in the Highlands
and the precursor of ice hockey in Canada. How it arrived in
California he doesn't explain, and the fact that it was played on
Sunday, after the church service, certainly was not part of Highland
tradition. A men's team played against a team of women. 'People
flocked in from all parts to see the sport, and heavy bets were made,'

Reid wrote. 'The priest took a great interest in the game, and as women seldom had less than half a dozen quarrels, in which hair flew by the handful, it pleased him very much.'

Reid was acutely aware of how drastically Native culture had been eroded by incoming Europeans, especially through the heavy hand of the Spanish missions. By the time he died, from tuberculosis in 1852 at the age of 42, California had been through a period of extraordinary upheaval, and had joined the USA. The gold rush had brought a massive influx of people, including many more Scots, but Hugo Reid was one of the first to have a real impact on the area, working as he did to improve treatment of Californian Natives, and contributing through trade, ranching and political activity to its economy and stability.

Community building in California was skewed by the repercussions of the gold rush, which in turn spilled over into adjacent territories and spread east and north. But gold was part of the foundation of San Francisco, and plenty of Scots would make their mark there. Some would be stunningly successful. Brothers Michael and Peter Donahoe, from Glasgow, after an abortive effort at prospecting for gold, started an iron foundry in San Francisco which made stoves and shovels for the miners. They were joined by a third brother, James. Peter Donahoe went on to set up a steamship company, build steam engines, start a quartz mill and found California's first printing press. He built the San Francisco and San Jose railway, became president of the Omnibus Railroad Company, and a director of the Hibernia Savings and Loan Society and the First National Gold Bank. He gave his name to the town of Donahoe in Sonoma County. A later arrival in San Francisco was Robert Dollar from Falkirk, whose fleet of cargo vessels plying up and down the coast was a prominent feature of Pacific shipping. He built up a shipping empire that by the 1920s extended to China, and he initiated the first round-the-world passenger service.

While some mining camps grew into substantial towns, and ports like San Francisco and Portland in Oregon boomed as a result, others died when lodes gave out and the excitement moved on to the location of the next discovery. When the miners left, the camp followers left too. The ghost town became a feature of the West. But for the mobile and the opportunistic another mine was another chance to make money, if not to find precious metal. Granville and James Stuart are good examples of Scottish pragmatism. By the 1880s the brothers had given up prospecting, and had turned to ranching in Montana. Some of their neighbours were also Scottish in origin: James Fergus, Robert Hamilton, C.D. Duncan, the Burnett brothers. Although, according to Stuart, cowboys were 'reluctant to obey any law but their own', the erosion of frontier latitude was inevitable as communities took root and the emblems of more conventional life became established. He reports his friend John Grant planting himself in Montana in a place that became Grantsville. 'We are becoming somewhat civilised as we remain long enough in one spot to give it a name.' Stuart, along with many of his fellow ranchers, contributed to the process of 'civilisation', although at times they found it more satisfactory to ignore the infrastructure they helped put in place. Their taxes went to build roads and schools 'and did much for the advancement of civilisation'. Like Stuart, many of them took on civic duties or became involved in politics. In 1882 Stuart was elected a member of the state legislative assembly.

Laurence Oliphant described, with a hint of ambivalence, what happened when people moved in to transform 'uncivilised regions'. He is writing about Wisconsin, but the relentlessness of the process is equally characteristic of points west. He writes of:

> The blind confidence which induces crowds of utterly destitute people to emigrate to comparatively unknown and altogether uncivilised regions, with the intention of living there permanently, – the cool presumption with which crowded steamers start for cities which do not exist, and disgorge their living freights upon lonesome and desolate shores, to shift for themselves, – and the

very remarkable manner in which they do shift for themselves –
first, by building a hotel, then a newspaper office, then probably
a Masonic lodge, or something equally unnecessary, then saloons
and places of entertainment – and, finally, shops and ordinary
dwelling-houses...

This description suggests something both inevitable and heroic,
and reflects the need for groups of people to replicate recognisable
features of civilised life. Survival in a lonely homestead was only
part of the story. Without communities and their functions the
West would not be won.

William Phillips from Paisley emigrated with his parents to
Illinois. By 1855 he was a lawyer in Kansas, where in 1858 he
founded the town of Salina. During the Civil War he commanded
the Cherokee Indian Regiment, and with the war over became
involved in politics. A Republican, he was elected to Congress three
times. Latterly, he was president of the Kansas Historical Society.
A rather more dubious contribution to the advance of civilisation
was the case of Scottish-born Jimmie Crain. He homesteaded on
the Yellowstone, and was a rancher, farmer and poker-player who
gave his name to a small town near Sidney, Montana. With minimal
education and no relevant experience, he was thrust into the role
of Justice of the Peace in Lone Tree, Nebraska, when his predecessor
was shot during a card game. His efforts to transform himself into
a respectable and respected citizen weren't entirely convincing.

As the mountain men had recognised decades earlier, frontier
freedoms were inevitably challenged by settlement. For Scots, church
and school were often priorities, and these became symbols of a
permanent community, counterpoising the saloon and the brothel
so often associated with the shifting populations of mining camps and
railheads. A.B. Guthrie in his memoir *The Blue Hen's Chick* (1965)
describes the small town of Choteau, Montana, in which he grew up,
with four saloons, one church and two general stores. In similar communities, Scottish names occur as storekeepers and blacksmiths

(Granville Stuart was both), essential occupations in areas as dependent on horses and tools as on supplies of provisions, seed and domestic equipment. The blacksmith in Wibaux, Montana was Bill Graham. His four daughters were described by John Leakey as having 'the biggest hearts in Montana'. One of the sisters ran a hotel with her husband, where 'no broke or hungry cowpuncher was ever turned away...without a meal under his belt'. John McIntosh opened a hardware store in Demersville in Montana's Flathead Valley, and followed that by building an opera house – perhaps the ultimate symbol of 'civilised' life.

Alexander Campbell McDougall, born in Edinburgh, emigrated with his family in the 1920s to Lander, Wyoming. Eventually he had his own store in Dubois, Idaho, on the Wind River. Fred Drummond, born in Ardrossan, Ayrshire, emigrated in 1884 and after an unsuccessful attempt at ranching in Texas with his brother, moved on to St Louis and then Oklahoma. He ran a store in Hominy selling 'general merchandise', which did well. He branched into banking and real estate, and then back to ranching. James Urquhart, born in Ferintosh, Ross-shire, had joined a wagon train on the Oregon Trail in the early 1850s. Once he was established, in Washington Territory, he sent for his wife and five children. He laid out the town of Napavine, farmed, went into business as a merchant, became county treasurer and postmaster, and was elected three times to the territory's legislature. All of these activities were part of the process of community building.

Scots were also found among lawyers and doctors. Dr Moses Macray moved with his family to New Albany, Kansas, and studied medicine at St Louis before becoming a doctor in Nebraska. Alexander McSween was a lawyer in Lincoln County, New Mexico, and played a prominent part in the Lincoln County War, in which the most famous protagonist was Billy the Kid. Richard Melrose left Scotland in 1864 and settled in Anaheim, California. As lawyer, politician, newspaper editor and philanthropist he played an important role in the developing community, and was notable for his support of equal rights for the large numbers of Japanese immigrants who were settling on the west coast. R.L. Brown was another lawyer, from Glasgow, who went to Austin, Texas in 1883, where he acted as agent for the Scottish American Mortgage Company and invested money in various land schemes.

A perception of Scots as particularly refined is implied in an anecdote quoted by Dee Brown. A cowhand called John Fox, a well-known practical joker, donned a dress and masqueraded as 'Miss Ferguson from Scotland'. 'I endeavoured to be very gracious, not to say condescending, and really succeeded in taking in one or two people for a few minutes,' he recounted. When the tie broke on his lace underskirt his cover was blown, and he made a hasty exit: '[I] reached my overalls and blue shirt from the back of the saddle, and changed back to a man again'. Mining camps and cattle towns were short of 'respectable' women and a feature of entertainment was men dancing together. It is easy to believe that the gracious 'Miss Ferguson' was quite a hit.

The transformation of a ramshackle frontier one-horse town into a real community was often signalled by the arrival of wives and children. A perennial theme of Westerns is the civilising influence of decent women, who set up homes with the appurtenances of respectable living – good furniture and drapery, glass and silverware, perhaps even a piano – and become pillars of church and school. Stuart and his fellow ranchers encouraged the setting up of schools: 'On our range whenever as many as six children could be assembled I provided a good log school house and a six months' term of school each year.' The British generally were often regarded as being better educated and more genteel than the average rough and ready American, and the Scots in particular were characterised as having a high regard for literacy and book learning, as well as being hard working and careful with money. Ivan Doig's memoir, *This House of Sky*, makes frequent reference to the latter as well as embodying the former. The young Doig, grandson of emigrant Scots and son of a peripatetic sheepman, reads avidly and is encouraged to go to college. He grows up with an appreciative awareness of his Scottish ancestry.

The necessary ingredient for a rooted community was a population. Even after the Civil War, when the numbers of emigrants travelling west increased dramatically, much of the frontier population was unstable. The career of Granville Stuart illustrates this vividly, as he moved from mining camp to mining camp before settling down as a rancher. Although acquisition of a cattle range gave him a firm location, his ranching depended on the hiring of cattlemen who also tended to be rootless. The frontier was characterised by the large numbers of people on the move, the classic drifter, moving from place to place looking for work, or simply too restless to stay in any one spot for long. But in Stuart's lifetime rough and ready cattle towns became substantial communities, and a contributory factor was the founding of organisations such as the Montana Stock Growers' Association in Miles City or the Wyoming Stock Growers in Cheyenne. They implied a degree of stasis. The membership of each of these associations included large numbers of Scots. The associations became a focus of social and political intercourse, and they leant a certain style and authority to local life.

If in an earlier phase of settlement the inducement to potential immigrants was the prospect of land and the scope for leading an independent life, the business opportunities offered by the West became an insistent theme. In 1857, Scot J.D. Borthwick wrote glowingly about his three years in California in a book published in Edinburgh:

> Every kind of business custom and employment was solicited with an importunity little known in old countries, where the course of all such things is so well worn and chanelled that it is not easily directed. But here the field was open and everyone was striving for what seemed to be within the reach of all – a foremost rank in his own sphere.

Alexander Craib echoed this view in a book published in Paisley

35 years later. There was, he wrote, 'a boundless inheritance in the west ... waiting our younger unsettled but aspiring sons who complain there is no room for them in our Scotland'. For many Scots responding to this invitation, the realities did not quite live up to the image. Running a general store in a Wyoming cattle town, setting up a tailor's business in Helena, Montana as did David Lawson Doig from Dundee before he took up ranching, or cooking for ranch crews like Annie Campbell from Perthshire, did not provide a route to riches.

At the heart of the frontier myth is violence of some kind, and at the heart of the civilising of the frontier was the bringing of law and order. Pioneers were encouraged to look after themselves. In A.B. Guthrie's *The Way West*, the wagon train is dependent on those with frontier skills, which of course include proficiency with weapons. Inevitably, weapons are misused – the gratuitous killing of a Kaw Indian by Curtis Mack (a Scottish name), for example – but they were considered part of everyday life, needed to protect and feed the family. Boys, and sometimes girls, were taught to shoot as a matter of course. When in Guthrie's darker novel *The Big Sky* the 17-year-old Boone leaves home, his most prized possession is the rifle he takes from his father. His mother says, 'I don't know what your pap'll do without that there rifle gun.' Weapons were an essential tool.

Boone's rifle is stolen and he is jailed on a trumped-up charge. He is found guilty at a rough-and-ready trial, but with the help of a friend manages to escape. Every frontier territory went through a period when maintaining the law was a haphazard affair, which offered plenty of opportunity for those inclined to bend or ignore legality. The Republic of Texas, being outwith the United States, attracted many who were escaping the law and had no intention of changing their ways. Violent contention over land and property was common. The three McFadden brothers, for example, in 1841 ambushed a man called Charles Jackson who was a key participant in a quarrel that had been raging in eastern Texas for some time.

Buckskin Bill McFadden then went on to dispatch Benjamin McClure (another Scottish name), the cousin of a man who revealed the names of Jackson's killers. The McFaddens were tracked down by a vigilante group known as the Regulators, and brought to the courthouse at Shelbyville, where the citizens voted unanimously to hang the brothers. The two older brothers, Buckskin Bill and Bailey, were duly hanged from the same tree. The youngest, Rufus, who was only 14, was given 20 lashes and ordered to leave town. It is difficult to believe that anything other than a criminal life lay ahead of him.

One of those who attempted to bring some order to eastern Texas was Judge William Ochiltree, who enlisted the help of Sam Houston to bring an end to anarchy in Shelby County. He was largely successful, although one of the Regulator leaders, Watt Moorman, was later killed by a doctor in Logansport called Robert Burns. In 1846 Judge Ochiltree moved on to Dallas, and set up his court in a log cabin. Trials took place under a tree. Between sessions, he played poker and conducted mock trials. In one of them, the jury fined Ochiltree two gallons of whisky for failing to attend a party that was the consequence of a previous whisky fine.

Texas wasn't exceptional. From the beginnings of the American colonies, criminal elements tended to ease west, beyond the reach of established communities and statutory law. The tendency continued, intensified by the Civil War which displaced large numbers of people, many of whom made their way west. Among them were discharged soldiers, especially those who had fought for the losing side, opportunists and misfits of various kinds, men and women who had grown accustomed to operating at the edge of what was legal, or beyond it. Numerous Scots were found on both sides of the law, and many others were among the citizens who felt justified in taking the law into their own hands.

William Graham was born in Missouri where he served an apprenticeship as a cattle rustler before heading for Texas and then New Mexico. There he became involved with the notorious

Clanton gang, big-time cattle thieves, and killed the first marshal of Tombstone, thus attracting the attention of Wyatt Earp. When other members of the gang were vanquished by Earp and his associates at the famous OK Corral gunfight (26 October 1881) Bill Graham was absent, although he vowed revenge. Twenty years later, another Graham, Dayton, was a law officer in Bisbee, Arizona. In a less celebrated gunfight, at Douglas, he was seriously injured by an outlaw called Bill Smith. It took Dayton Graham many months to track down Smith. When he eventually found him in a saloon, both men simultaneously reached for their guns and when the smoke cleared Smith was dead.

A young man called Jack McCall left his Kentucky home in the late 1860s to join buffalo hunters on the prairies. In 1876 he appeared in Deadwood, South Dakota, calling himself Sutherland. On the afternoon of 2 August he walked into Deadwood's No. 10 Saloon where four men were playing poker. The man with his back to McCall was pondering his hand of aces and eights. He usually made a point of facing the door, but this time he wasn't in his favoured seat. McCall approached him, drew a rather antiquated Colt .45, and fired a shot into the back of his head. McCall tried to escape but was quickly apprehended. He had just brought to an end the life of James Butler Hickok, otherwise known as Wild Bill. There were no legal officials in Deadwood and no law court, but the day after the murder local citizens tried McCall. In his defence, he argued that he had shot Hickok in revenge for the killing of his brother, and was acquitted. When asked 'Why didn't you go around in front of Wild Bill and shoot him like a man?', he allegedly replied, 'I didn't want to commit suicide.'

While he was being tried, the funeral of Wild Bill was taking place, attended by a substantial crowd. Captain Jack Crawford, the Scottish American 'poet scout', commemorated the occasion in verse:

You buried him 'neath the old pine tree,
  In that little world of ours,
His trusty rifle by his side –
  His grave all strewn with flowers;
His manly form in sweet repose,
  That lovely silken hair –
I tell you, pard, it was a sight,
  That face so white and fair!

Hickok was 39, and for 15 years had been a professional gunman, operating on both sides of the law. There were plenty of people with a grudge against him, who considered that McCall had done them a service, but McCall's actual motive remains a mystery; the brother was fictitious.

McCall left Deadwood for Laramie, but couldn't resist the adulation and free drinks he encountered in the Laramie saloons. Overheard boasting of how he had fooled the Deadwood jury, he was arrested by a deputy US marshal and eventually tried back in Dakota Territory. The Federal Judge was called Blair. This time, a verdict of guilty was delivered, and Jack McCall was duly hanged on 1 March 1877 at Yankton. A few days before his execution the Yankton marshal received a letter, signed Mary A. McCall. It was from Jack's mother. She had read in a newspaper that Wild Bill Hickok had been shot by a man called Jack McCall:

> There was a young man of the name of John McCall left here about six years ago, who has not been heard from for the last three years. He has a father, mother, and three sisters living here in Louisville, who are very uneasy about him since they heard about the murder of Wild Bill. If you can send us any information about him, we would be thankful to you.

Mary McCall's letter opens a small window onto the families of the youngsters who lit out for the West. Most we know nothing of. Apart from their Scottish name, we know nothing of the origins of the McCalls, how they came to be in Louisville, why Jack left home or what led him to murder one of the legends of the West. They have, nevertheless, become part of the mainstream of American – and Scottish – history.

Although McCall's defence was spurious, revenge killings were common. Hugh Anderson pursued Mike McCluskie, the killer of a friend, and shot him in a bloody gun battle in which Anderson himself was wounded. Then he in turn became the target of McCluskie's brother, who caught up with him in Medicine Lodge, Kansas. In the ensuing gun duel the two men wounded each other with pistols, then attacked with knives. Neither of them survived.

James Stuart appeared in California in 1850, by way of a spell as a convict in Australia. He re-commenced his criminal career, as a robber and horse thief, and then as a murderer. He was arrested by San Francisco vigilantes, a large and well-organised band formed to combat the increasing number of robberies and killings in the town, which seethed with a criminal underworld. Stuart was convicted and summarily hanged. As described in Wayne Gard's book *Frontier Justice* (1949):

> At the Market Street wharf, the loose end of the vigilante rope was thrown over a derrick and seized by a score of hands. While the men in the crowd bared their heads and those on ships in the harbour raised their flags and fired their cannons, eager executioners jerked the prisoner into the air. After he had swung for half an hour before the crowd, his body was lowered and turned over to the coroner.

This was, of course, contrary to the rule of law. The man who had to deal with it was Governor John McDougal, but he supported the vigilance committee and did no more than issue a rather limp proclamation asking citizens not to take part in unlawful acts. But there were those who were critical of the vigilantes, among them Judge Alexander Campbell of the Court of Session. He condemned the hanging and attempted to indict those responsible, but the jury, which included two vigilantes and several sympathisers, refused to do so. There was clearly popular support for vigilante action. The San Francisco *Herald* asked: 'Whenever the law becomes an empty name, has not the citizen the right to supply its deficiency?'

At least three Scots, and probably more among the 900 who made up the vigilante band, were involved in this one episode. But it wasn't the end of the story. Associates of James Stuart were Robert McKenzie and a man called Gibson, who may also have been a Scot. The two men had arrived in California, like Stuart after a sojourn in Australia. The vigilantes apprehended both of them and prepared for a hanging. This time, Governor McDougal intervened, and the prisoners were taken into official custody. Not for long. The San Francisco vigilantes were convinced, or so they claimed, that the two men would be acquitted if left to due process, and stormed the jail in which they were held, having first lured the sheriff away to a local bullfight. McKenzie and Gibson were quickly taken to the vigilance committee's headquarters in Battery Street, and immediately hanged.

R.L. Stevenson, in San Francisco in 1879 and 1880, was uncomfortably aware of the violence on the streets: 'I saw a man standing watchfully at a street corner with a long Smith-and-Wesson glittering in his hand behind his back.' Vengeance and extravagance existed cheek by jowl. The vigilance committee met in the Palace Hotel, 'the world's greatest caravanserai, served by lifts and lit by electricity; where in the great glazed court a band nightly discourses music from a grove of palms. So do extremes meet in this city of contrasts.'

There were vigilance committees all over California and other parts of the West, often because statutory law enforcement was non-existent or because officials were perceived as, and clearly often were, inefficient and corrupt. After the triple hangings of 1851 there were a few years which saw a decline of crime in San Francisco and more rigorous official attempts to deal with what there was. But by 1855 the situation had deteriorated, and there was again a call for direct action. The *Herald* looked back to 'the good and vigorous days of the vigilance committee'.

But these days were not over, as vigilante action followed the criminal trail of the mining camps and railheads. In Leadville, Colorado, in 1879, an outlaw called Patrick Stewart and another armed man held up a local barber. But the barber was armed and retaliated, wounding Stewart and killing his companion. Stewart was arrested and jailed. Leadville citizens were not content to allow the law to take its course. A group of vigilantes forced the deputy sheriff to let them into the jail, removed Stewart and another gunman from their cells, and hanged them.

In the Montana mining camps vigilante groups were also active, although gestures were made towards appointing law officers. In 1863 Bannack had a population of around a thousand, mostly miners and those who fed off miners, and, according to historian Wayne Gard, 'a bigger crew of outlaws than almost any other town of its size'. Bannack was a long way from becoming a 'civilised' community. Many people were living in the wagons that had brought them there, as there were not enough houses. 'With the prospectors had come gamblers, bandits, and dance-hall girls to relieve the miners of their gold dust and nuggets. As Montana did not yet have even a territorial government, there was almost no curb on lawless activities.' For a short time they had a sheriff, a butcher called Hank Crawford, who lasted for two months. After wounding an outlaw called Henry Plummer, who vowed vengeance, he beat a diplomatic retreat back east to Wisconsin. Shortly afterwards, the citizenry of Bannack elected Plummer as their sheriff, which gave him ample opportunity to pursue his criminal activities. Vigilantes finally caught up with him, and he and five of his henchmen were hanged.

Another Scottish American lawman seemed to have decided that discretion was the better part of valour. James McDonald was deputy marshal in Abilene, Kansas, which in 1870 was a booming cow town with the usual problems of keeping the peace. One of many quarrels and confrontations arose when Andrew McConnell shot a neighbour whom he found driving cattle across his land. The neighbour attempted to fire at him first. McConnell went for a doctor and gave himself up, pleading self-defense. He was released, but not everyone was satisfied with this outcome, and Tom Smith, us marshal, with his deputy James McDonald set off to apprehend McConnell. In the ensuing affray, Smith was shot by McConnell and a companion, and McDonald abandoned him, taking off back to Abilene for help. Although McConnell was later caught and jailed, Smith died. Many years later, in 1904, Abilene erected a memorial to Smith, which stated that he was 'a fearless hero of frontier days, who in cowboy chaos, established the supremacy of law'. The rather less fearless McDonald is not mentioned.

The vigilante tradition continued when ranching spread in Montana. Horse thieves were considered to be fair game. The Judith River region saw several horse thieves dispatched in the summer of 1884. One of them was a man called Sam McKenzie, part Indian, who was stealing horses in Montana and taking them over the border to sell in Canada, where he stole Canadian horses to dispose of in the us. He was caught with two stolen horses by local ranch hands near Fort Maginnis, and 'hanged from the limb of a cottonwood tree', as Granville Stuart recorded. Stuart himself was reputedly an instigator of vigilante action, and organised a band of men known as 'Stuart's Stranglers'. He doesn't admit to this in his memoir, indeed denies that Montana cattlemen hired gunmen to track down horse thieves and rustlers, but he does describe a number of incidents.

There was, for example, the occasion when a vigilante posse intercepted a us marshal who was escorting four captured horse thieves. The posse relieved him of his prisoners and hanged them from a log supported by cabin roofs. The hanging accomplished, the cabins were burnt down. Stuart's description of tracking down two suspicious characters could come straight from a Western:

Both men were armed, each wearing two 44 Colt revolvers and a hunting knife. When I rode into their camp, ['Rattle Snake Jake' Fallon] was sitting on a roll of blankets cleaning a Winchester rifle. Owen was reclining against a stump smoking and another Winchester lay on a coat within easy reach. Owen was self-possessed, almost insolent, 'Rattle Snake Jake' was civil but nervously tinkered with the gun and kept his eyes on me all the time I was in their camp.

Shortly afterwards, during Fourth of July celebrations, Rattle Snake Jake shot a man. Citizens opened fire, and killed both Jake and Owen. If Stuart was among those citizens, he does not say.

When Malcolm Campbell arrived in Cheyenne, Wyoming, in 1868, he witnessed in quick succession four vigilante hangings, demonstrating, so he wrote, 'the strength of the law, and the impotence of the criminal'. Later, he became well known as a sheriff. 'Undoubtedly,' he said, 'these incidents went far in shaping my future life and in guiding my feet properly in those trails of danger where I was later to apprehend some of the most dangerous outlaws of the plains.' Vigilantism readily elided into legitimate law enforcement, and the latter could not always escape the tradition of instant retribution, especially when there could be a long wait for the courts to catch up with alleged criminals.

Personal vengeance is a recurrent theme in Westerns. In Clint Eastwood's *High Plains Drifter* it is a whole town that is punished for standing by when Marshal Jim Duncan is savagely murdered. Duncan is not the only Scottish name among the townspeople, dead or alive. The Stranger (who, the end of the film implies, is Duncan's vengeance-seeking ghost) rides into town through a graveyard where the name 'Scott' is conspicuous on a grave marker. He proceeds down the main street past the name 'Ross' on a storefront. Whether the Scottish allusions were intended or accidental is hard to say, but the notions of hell, Satan and retribution that the film evokes have a strikingly Calvinist resonance.

In all the attempts to bring order to frontier society, no name was more resonant in the second half of the 19th century than that of Pinkerton. Allan Pinkerton and his wife Joan Carfrae left Glasgow in 1842, and set up a cooperage business in Dundee, Illinois. Within a few years Pinkerton was deputy sheriff of Cook County, before in 1850 being appointed Chicago's first detective. His own private detective agency followed. With the post-Civil War spread of population and the railroads forging west there was an increasing demand for the protection of property as well as the apprehension of criminals. Pinkerton recruited men who worked all over the US, and were prominent in tracking down in particular the bandits who preyed on the railroads west of the Mississippi.

Two of the most notorious gangs of outlaws, operating mainly in Missouri, were the James and Younger gangs (both names that could be Scots, though this has not been established). Jesse and Frank James and Cole, Jim and John Younger all cut their teeth riding with Charles Quantrill, leader of a Missouri pro-slavery guerilla band that marauded across the border in Kansas and further afield, before and during the Civil War. Missouri and 'bleeding' Kansas, as it became known, were the arena of savage fighting between irregulars, with Quantrill's particularly bloody raid in 1863 on Lawrence, Kansas the apogee. After the Civil War, the James and Younger brothers continued their marauding habits, claiming that Union antagonism made it impossible for them to settle down. They robbed banks and trains, and evaded capture for years largely because family and well-wishers sheltered them, and law officers were afraid to act.

The Pinkerton Agency was brought in when Missouri got desperate about the ravaging of the state by outlaws. In March 1872 the Youngers shot one Pinkerton operative, and possibly a second, whose body was found riddled with bullets. In the gun battle, a local sheriff, Ed Daniels, and John Younger also lost their lives, and Jim Younger was wounded. The doctor who treated the dying Daniels was Dr D.C. McNeil. In the winter of 1875 the Pinkertons, with a posse of locals, attacked the farmhouse of the James brothers' mother and stepfather. In the fracas Jesse's mother had her arm torn off and his young step-brother was killed. As a consequence Jesse's hatred for Allan Pinkerton and his son William, also involved in the business, was intense. In his determination to kill Allan Pinkerton he trailed him to Chicago, but in the event decided that 'to shoot him down would be too swift'. He wanted to watch him die.

'So great is the terror that the Jameses and the Youngers have instilled in Clay County that their names are never mentioned save in backrooms and then only in a whisper,' commented the *Missouri World*. The St Louis Midland Railroad offered rewards for the arrest of Jesse and Frank James. The Younger brothers were arrested after a James–Younger raid on the First National Bank of Northfield, Minnesota, when citizens intervened and fought off the outlaws. (This is the episode which features in the many films based on the James and Younger brothers.) Jesse was famously dispatched on 3 April 1882 by Bob Ford, tempted by a $10,000 reward. Seven months later Frank gave himself up, and stood trial for the murder of a train conductor and a passenger called McMillan. The prosecutor in the trial was William Wallace. Frank Younger was acquitted and lived on until 1915, when he died in his step-father's Missouri farmhouse.

Allan Pinkerton himself and his son William were involved in on-the-ground detective work. Allan pursued Frank Reno of the Reno gang into Canada and William trailed the Farrington brothers, who had also ridden with Quantrill, and fought a moonlight gun battle with Hilary Farrington on the deck of a steamboat. William was spared having a killing on his hands as Farrington slipped and went over the side, to be crushed by the paddle. Several Pinkerton operatives were Scottish Americans, among them Frank Murray who worked particularly on train robbery cases.

Most of the well-known Western outlaws were on the Pinkerton books. One of Pinkerton's successful innovations was the keeping of detailed records and descriptions of wanted men. Among them was Harvey Logan of the Wild Bunch. His file includes observations on his personality: 'Reserved manner. Drinks heavy, and has bad habits.' A long list of crimes is recorded: murders (including four sheriffs and deputies), bank and train robberies and jail break-outs, in South Dakota, Montana, Wyoming, Colorado, Utah, Arizona, Texas and Tennessee. He was one of those who, along with Butch Cassidy, held up a Union Pacific train at Wilcox, Wyoming. They used dynamite to blow up the safe, and shredded bonds and currency in the process, a scene dramatised in George Roy Hill's film *Butch Cassidy and the Sundance Kid* (1969). This was only one of a series of train robberies that had Pinkerton men and others pursuing members of the Wild Bunch all over the West and finally into South America. After yet another train robbery in Colorado, Logan was hunted down, and shot himself to avoid capture. When news of a dead and buried criminal reached the Pinkerton office in Denver, Detective McParland was sure it was Harvey Logan, but William Pinkerton issued an order to have the corpse dug up and properly identified. It was eventually confirmed that Logan was indeed no more.

In *Butch Cassidy and the Sundance Kid* the Pinkerton men on the trail of Butch and Sundance are portrayed as faceless and sinister, relentless in their pursuit of the two heroes. The Pinkertons did not give up. The business of detection and pursuit was organised and systematic, and Allan and William Pinkerton were quick to make use of improved communications – the telegraph, then the telephone – as well as the railways which were so often a criminal target, to help them get their man. Pinkerton men were also widely used as strike-breakers and to quell industrial unrest, which earned them intense unpopularity.

For all the efforts to make the transition to law-abiding, conventional communities, lawlessness was still endemic in the West in the 1890s. The Doolin gang terrorised the Oklahoma badlands, and 17-year-old Annie McDougal, smitten by one of the gang members, decided to join them. She gained a reputation as 'Cattle Annie', a horse and cattle thief who wore men's clothes, was a good shot with a Winchester, and sold bootleg whisky. The law caught up with her, and her sidekick Jennie 'Little Britches' Stevens, and they were dispatched east to a Boston penitentiary. When they arrived at the railroad station there was a huge crowd agog to set eyes on 'Oklahoma's girl bandits'. They were released after two years, and Cattle Annie returned to Pawnee, north of Guthrie, where she married and led a respectable life.

Annie McDougal made the transition to respectability, but many frontier people found it very difficult, and Western literature is full of drifters, men and women who cannot settle down and feel there is no place for them in a conventional community. For those who strove to establish themselves and the places where they lived as law-abiding and properly regulated, gestures and tokens were often of great importance. Mary McGee came to Tombstone, Arizona in 1884, with her mining engineer husband. When relatives at home in Scotland sent her roses and other Scottish shrubs, she planted them alongside the inn where the couple stayed until their own house was ready. The roses flourished and spread, and a large rose garden survives as a legacy.

Scots transplanted not just roses but old country ways and traditions. Caledonian Clubs, Burns Clubs and St Andrews Societies emerged all over the United States, and the West was no exception. In December 1882, the *Denver Republican* reported on the local Caledonian Club Ball: 'If any people know how to enjoy themselves it's the Scotch.' The paper acknowledged the Scots could be clannish, but that 'a people coming from a country so rich in historical reminiscences have a right to be'. Scottish romanticism and Caledonian balls may appear to sit uneasily in an environment where outlawry, feuding and vigilantism were commonplace, but the survival of the folk traditions which underpinned the retention of a Scottish identity was part of the fabric of migration.

Much of what Scots contributed to the developing communities of the West is illusive. The Scottish legacy that Ivan Doig expresses in *This House of Sky* suggests that the Scots brought with them a ruggedness and persistence which were vital to survival in a hard country, as well as a regard for education and values of decency. Doig uses words like 'flinty' and 'stubborn'. When he describes a Montana rancher called McTaggart as 'a high crag of a man, wintry, boulder-jawed, long-boned, who had been battling the northern plains for half a century' he could be portraying a Highland Scot. He records an existence populated by Scottish homesteaders such as the Stewarts and the Christisons who 'formed a kind of trestle of relatives and fellow Scots' which provides a focus of support and identity. A Scots cadence and what R.L. Stevenson described as 'a strong Scotch accent of the mind' survive in the speech of his father. In many ways these mountain communities portrayed by Doig survived as they did because people like the Doigs sustained their frontier skills and stuck it out. Community building was an aspect of survival, rather than a conscious effort at 'civilised' living.

CHAPTER 9

Range War

Way out in the West when the country was young
And the gun was your law and your law was the gun.

'Billy the Kid', traditional, as sung by Woody Guthrie

WHEN THE CIVIL WAR came to an end, 27,000 square miles of unfenced grazing land in Lincoln County, New Mexico, were attracting not only cattlemen and honest settlers, but misfits and outlaws of all descriptions. With law enforcement in Texas becoming more effective, many crossed the border into New Mexico looking for fresh marauding opportunities. This did not prevent John Simpson Chisum, 'King of the Pecos', from consolidating a cattle empire around his Jingle-Bob Ranch, but by the mid 1870s rustling was an increasing problem, and the small-scale homesteaders were identified as the perpetrators.

Chisum believed the homesteaders threatened his cattle range and helped themselves to his cattle. In the eyes of the homesteaders, Chisum was a cattle baron whose claim to public land was shaky and whose vast herds could seamlessly absorb their own stock. It was a situation that was repeated in many parts of the West over a period of around twenty years, and was resolved with varying degrees of violence and recrimination. In some cases, it wasn't really resolved at all. Accounts of range war and clashes between big ranchers and small homesteaders often feature Scottish names. It must have reminded some of the clan warfare of the past.

The Lincoln County War, as it came to be known, may have had its origins in rustling and local quarrels over land, but it evolved into a contest between two rival factions, the Scottish American Chisum on the one hand, and the Irish American Major L.G. Murphy and J.J. Dolan on the other. Major Murphy owned a general store in Lincoln, about half way between the Pecos River and the Rio Grande, which cut through New Mexico north to south. Murphy had a lucrative government contract to supply beef to local Indian reservations, and he also ran a banking operation. Suspecting that some of Murphy's beef was purloined from the Jingle-Bob, Chisum set out to catch the rustlers red-handed. Murphy had hired a lawyer called Alexander McSween (an Argyll name) from Kansas. McSween was a man of religious convictions who carried a bible in his saddlebag; when he refused to defend the rustlers, he was promptly sacked by Murphy.

McSween got together with an English ranch owner called John Tunstall and they set up a rival general store, which was supported by Chisum. Among the men working for Tunstall was a teenager called William Bonney, born in New York, raised in Kansas, who had previously been employed by Murphy. There had been sporadic eruptions of violence for two years when, in February 1878, Tunstall was waylaid and killed by two Murphy men called Frank Baker and Billy Morton (a Scottish name). Bonney, better known as Billy the Kid, had grown attached to Tunstall, who had befriended the 'rough, untamed, homeless child of the frontier' (as described by historians James Horan and Paul Sann), and vowed revenge. Within a month, Baker and Morton, and a third man called McCloskey, were all dead, dispatched by Billy with the help of Frank McNab, foreman on Chisum's South Spring Ranch and member of a posse organised by McSween. Billy didn't stop there. He also shot the sheriff and his deputy, who were Murphy men. McNab was another casualty, killed outside Lincoln by the Murphy gang.

A furious Murphy organised a rival gang to lay siege to Alexander McSween's house in Lincoln. A gunfight between the besiegers and the Chisum/McSween faction in the house lasted for three days, with no resolution. The situation got so bad that troops were sent for, but they were unable to prevent the besiegers setting the house alight and shooting McSween as he attempted to escape the flames. Billy, also in the house, got away, having first shot the man who killed McSween. Lincoln County was in turmoil, and the reverberations were felt in Washington when local ranchers called on newly elected President Hayes (son of an Ulster Scot) to sort things out. He responded by appointing Lew Wallace (another Scottish name) as governor of New Mexico. Wallace would make his name as author of *Ben Hur*, which he was working on at the time.

The situation worsened. A lawyer hired by Alexander McSween's widow was killed by three gunmen, one of whom was called William Campbell. Billy the Kid was a witness, and attempted to do a deal with Governor Wallace, whereby he would turn state's evidence in return for a pardon. Billy gave himself up, but understanding that the pardon would not in fact be granted, he absconded before his case came up for trial. He had entered the final chapter of his short life. A few months later Pat Garrett was elected sheriff of Lincoln County and was on Billy's trail. Billy in the meantime managed to gun down an inebriated Joe Grant who had made no secret of the fact that he intended to do away with the Kid. When Pat Garrett finally caught up with him, he arrested Billy, who was duly tried and convicted, but escaped the gallows by killing the two deputies who were guarding him. Garrett went after him again, this time tracking him down to a house owned by Peter Maxwell (a Scottish Borders name) where he shot and killed the 21-year-old outlaw on 14 July 1881.

The Lincoln County War is a tale of rivalry and revenge, ambush and murder, epitomising the greed and ruthlessness that flourished on the frontier, and the fragility of attempts to enforce the law. It has powerful echoes of 16th and 17th century Scottish Border warfare, where reivers with names like Elliot and Armstrong, Graham and Maxwell, contended in a no-man's-land that seemed impossible to police. It has echoes, too, of the warring clans in the Highlands, where cattle thieving was endemic and fierce family loyalties underpinned a culture of violence. For centuries, the Highlands and the Scottish Borders were beyond the reach of

Edinburgh and even less controllable by London, just as America's moving frontier always seemed to operate independently of Washington. The situations were similar, and some of the *dramatis personae* were in effect the same.

The Chisholms came originally from Strathglass near Inverness. In the 18th century 'Memoriall anent the true state of the Highlands' the chieftain of the clan was described as being able to 'bring out 200 men'. John Chisum's hired guns were not quite in the same category, but Chisum did seem to command a degree of loyalty, and, in some interpretations at least, echoes the paternalism of the clans. The Campbells were a widespread and influential Highland clan, with their power base in Argyll. The Grants were a Speyside family, and the McNabs came from Glendochart. If heather-covered Highland hills and swift running rivers had little in common with the dry canyons and broad rivers of New Mexico, the habits of uncompromising independent action flourished in both terrains. In the United States, the frontier values which offered land to all those with modest funds and an appetite for hard work soon clashed with an individualist ethic which rewarded the determinedly – and often ruthlessly – acquisitive. Scots undoubtedly played a part in this, on both sides of the barbed wire fences that were increasingly intruding on the landscape; the role call of Scottish names in the Lincoln County War is striking.

The Lincoln County War is the subject of several Westerns, notably – in terms of its focus on Chisum, if not of quality – the movie directed by Andrew McLaglen called *Chisum* (1970). In it, John Wayne is John Chisum, encapsulating much of what characterises the frontier hero. Chisum presides over his cattle empire with paternalistic firmness. He is a pioneer who has worked hard to acquire and hold land and cattle, and has a high regard for frontier skills and courage. He respects the local Apaches, and is decent to his struggling Mexican neighbours. A good citizen, when the Murphy consortium puts up prices, he opens a store which stocks affordable goods. The local populace reveres him and would die for him.

In McLaglen's version, Chisum has earned this loyalty, through his courage and his belief in justice – even if it is justice as enacted by himself rather than officers of the law. It is too important, he believes, to be left to the sheriff, and indeed it took a long time for the law to be brought to bear in the Lincoln County fracas. What *Chisum* demonstrates is the way sturdy individualism, so valued on the frontier, easily morphs into corporate values. If John Chisum had visited the Highlands of his relatives he might have found something similar. There, too, in the 1870s vast acreages were presided over by individuals, though in their case it was likely to have been cash rather than hard graft that acquired the land. Clan loyalty paradoxically often survived the bruising and erosion that came with the introduction of modern farming methods and pressure to make Highland estates pay, and the inability and often unwillingness of chieftains and landowners to sustain their side of the traditional bargain. Many, rather than caring for clan members, saw them as impediments to progress which had to be removed. The real Chisum viewed Apaches in much the same light. Some big ranch owners, whose claim to their land was in some cases as dubious as that of Highland landowners, regarded anyone who occupied 'their' space as an illegitimate presence.

While the Lincoln County drama was being played out, dominated then and later by the life and death of young William Bonney, in Gila County, Arizona, another contest was taking place. The neighbouring ranching families of Graham and Tewksbury settled in the Tonto Basin in the early 1880s, and although they at first seemed to get on well, arguments arose over cattle running on the other's range, and sporadic confrontations followed. The animosity intensified when the Tewksburys turned to sheep, to the disgust of the Grahams. The feud came to a head when the Tewksbury brothers and their gunmen ambushed cowboys working for the Grahams, leaving three dead and two wounded. Then 22-year-old William Graham was shot. The Grahams retaliated, attacking the Tewksbury ranch; John Tewksbury was killed. This unleashed five years of savage violence against men and beasts. Sheep were driven over cliff edges and a Navajo herder was beheaded. Locals not involved in the quarrel felt compelled to leave the area. Each time it seemed that the feud had come to an end there was another eruption of violence. The last surviving Graham brother, John, was shot down by two horsemen in 1892. Ed Tewksbury was arrested and tried in Tucson, and although he spent two-and-a-half years in jail the charges against him were eventually dismissed.

Like the Lincoln County War, the Graham-Tewksbury feud provided the theme for several Westerns. Amelia Bean's novel *The Feud* was filmed in 1919, and starred Tom Mix, himself with a Scottish Cherokee mother. Dane Coolidge's *The Man Killers* was also based on the feud, but better known is Zane Grey's *To the Last Man*, which was filmed twice. Victor Fleming directed it in 1923, Henry Hathaway 10 years later, with Randolph Scott.

Animosity on the part of cattle ranchers towards sheep and their shepherds was widespread. John Minto, one of the original Scottish American overlanders, raised sheep on his Oregon land. His comment was that 'during the years of expansion of the sheep industry over the portion of Oregon west of the Blue Mountains, more lives have been taken and more property destroyed over range feuds, provided by a marauding spirit, than by the racial wars with the natives.' As late as 1917, unidentified attackers killed the 2,000-strong flock of Colorado sheep farmer John Campbell.

It is not surprising, then, that as well as the re-workings of the Graham-Tewksbury confrontations, the rivalry between cattlemen and sheepherders makes a frequent appearance in Westerns, and because Scottish shepherds (and their dogs) were so important a feature of Western sheep farming, they have a place in the fiction-alised versions. It is interesting that in the 21st century Western, *Brokeback Mountain*, based on the story by Annie Proulx (in *Close Range: Wyoming Stories*, 1999), it is sheep that the 'cow-boys' are herding.

The pressure on land and the spread of fencing, which could

cut homesteaders and ranchers off from water as well as prevent access to grazing, ensured that range wars continued, on a small and large scale, well into the 1890s. The Scottish-owned XIT Ranch in Texas enclosed grasslands around the size of the state of Connecticut, using 6,000 miles of wire. Another Scottish ranch, the Spur, erected a fence that was 57 miles long. In the mid-1880s 10 wagonloads of barbed wire were shipped to the Matador Ranch. Scottish-born Thomas Carson, representative of the Scottish Mortgage and Land Investment Company in New Mexico, boasted of having enclosed public land on which he paid no rent. Barbed wire was, according to historians Hugh Graham and Ted Gurr, 'savage, unrefined, cruel, and hard'. Fence-cutting conflict was equally savage: 'people were killed, property destroyed, business crippled, and otherwise peaceful citizens alienated from one another'.

It is a feature of frontier history that apparently anachronistic confrontations continued well after the arrival of electricity and the telephone and even the motor car. (Indeed, it could be argued that they have never gone away.) The apparent incongruity of a frontier ethos existing alongside the infrastructure of respectability is highlighted by what is perhaps the best known of the West's range feuds, the Johnson County War.

By 1890, Wyoming had recovered to some extent from the devastating winters of 1885–6 and 1886–7, and the big cattle ranchers had regained confidence. In theory, 80 per cent of the land was still public domain. In practice, the big ranchers resented the encroachment of homesteaders, and accused them of helping themselves to animals not their own. There was a basis of truth in their accusations. Cattle did disappear. It wasn't difficult to pilfer an unbranded calf or slaughter a steer and destroy the evidence – the hide with its identifying brand. But rustling was now on a scale that was making serious inroads into ranchers' profits. 'There are too many people here now,' complained the Secretary of the Board of Live Stock Commissioners in 1892, 'too many people and not enough cattle.' Stock detectives were hired, Pinkerton men brought in, and gunmen deployed in efforts to halt the rustling. Homesteaders were threatened, and on occasion killed. Some people simply disappeared. In Johnson County, in the Powder River country, the situation was particularly bad.

John Clay describes how the rustling was done:

> Away out on divides, on crisp winter days, or in snug valleys sheltered by box elders, cottonwoods, or willows, a couple of cowboys came across a bunch of cattle. They would gently circle them, and their practised eye would soon detect unbranded calves. If they were following their mother, and were big enough, they would take their chances and treat them as mavericks [unbranded cattle which could be claimed by anyone]. They singled a maverick or big calf out of the bunch, and getting a run on him or her, the rope shot out swift and generally sure. It took only a minute or two to tie the animal down, a fire was lit, and the little branding iron carried in their 'chaps' was heated. They traced their brand on its hide, possibly slit its tongue, and they had added another animal to their book count.

Cattle-rustling was both a small-scale sideline, with individuals killing a steer to feed their families or branding unmarked calves as described by Clay, and also an organised business on a much larger scale. Harvey Logan and the Hole in the Wall gang were among the professionals. Many people were implicated in stealing cattle who were not necessarily rustlers themselves. Ella Watson, known as 'Cattle Kate', allegedly accepted rustled cattle in payment for personal services – according to Clay she was 'the common property of the cowboys for miles around'. Close associates were Jim Averill (reputedly a graduate of Cornell University) and his foreman Frank Buchanan (a Stirlingshire name). Averill took up a claim near the village of Bothwell (a Scottish Borders name) in the Sweetwater valley, where he opened a store and saloon frequented by local ranchers and cowboys. He became a leading voice in the protests of small ranchers against the Stock Grower's Association, which had backed a law declaring that all mavericks should be rounded up and sold, the proceeds going to the Association. The big ranchers became increasingly suspicious at the growing number of cattle in his and Cattle Kate's corrals, and when Averill contested possession of land claimed by cattlemen, the latter decided to act.

In July 1889, a group of 10 horsemen arrived at the adjoining homesteads of Averill and Cattle Kate, and arrested them. Frank Buchanan made a single-handed attempt to release them, but was forced to retreat. The pair were taken by wagon to a gully on the Sweetwater and hanged from a cottonwood tree. It was, said Clay, 'a horrible piece of business' but he was prepared to justify it: 'Are you to sit still and see your property ruined with no redress in sight?'

In a piece called 'The Fate of a Cattle Rustler' (published as a booklet in 1910), John Clay gives another account of retribution exacted on cattle rustlers. He and Al Bowie, superintendent of the Swan Ranch, with Tom Horn, a range detective and notorious gunman 'with sinews of steel, nerves of iron, the cunning of a fox, the pertinacity of a hound', caught red-handed a rustler called Sullivan. He was arrested, and tried in Cheyenne three months later, in front of Judge Scott. The foreman of the jury was Scot Johnnie Gordon, known as the Wyoming poet, who persuaded a reluctant jury to convict. He is reported to have said: 'Aye, aye, men, if ye dinna convict, waur things may happen.' Sullivan was sentenced to three years, but escaped before he could be locked up, and in spite of a reward of $1,000 was never caught. Years later Clay was told by a friend of Sullivan's that he had found him dead, an apparent suicide, and had destroyed the evidence by setting fire to the cabin where his corpse was lying.

According to Clay, although there were hundreds of arrests for horse- and cattle-stealing, judges and juries were 'friendly to all classes of crime', and it was very difficult to get a conviction. Clay himself, with another Scottish American called Jimmy Craig, took part in an abortive episode to track down an alleged rustler. The following year Clay engaged George Henderson, also a Scottish name, 'a silent, shrewd, able man ... a born sleuth' who had been a Pinkerton agent. 'He would rather hunt a thief than eat,' commented Clay. Craig and Henderson pursued a horse thief to Idaho and brought him back to Lander, Wyoming, but Clay doesn't relate what happened to him. Henderson himself was later shot 'by a rustler'.

In 1892 members of the Wyoming Stock Growers Association, based in Cheyenne, decided to take matters into their own hands. It is not difficult to imagine heated discussion over cigars and brandy in the comfortable surroundings of the Cheyenne Club, a favourite gathering place of influential ranchers. Leading characters in the drama were Frank Wolcott, a former US Army major who had fought in the Civil War, and Frank Canton, a gunfighter from Texas. Wolcott ranched on Deer Creek, near the town of Glenrock on the North Platte. Clay describes him as 'the gallant Major ... a fire-eater, honest, clean, a rabid Republican with a complete absence of tact, very well educated and a most delightful companion'. But he conceded that he was feared and hated by many. Canton was said to be obsessed by guns and killing, although that isn't the impression he gives in his own memoir, *Frontier Trails* (1930). In it he describes the activities of the rustlers, and says that stolen cattle were sold on to a merchant in Buffalo, an unnamed 'Scotchman who had made a fortune in the early days in Wyoming...on tie contracts with the Union Pacific Railroad Company'. He bought the cattle cheap, but when he shipped them to market in Omaha the blotched brands were noticed by the stock inspectors and the cattle were confiscated.

Wolcott and Canton may have been the most prominent of those who took action, but many Scots (including Clay, although he was out of the country when events reached their climax) were implicated in the next stage of the campaign against Wyoming rustlers, which now took on the character of a military operation. It was carefully planned and almost certainly there were some in fairly high places who knew what the intentions were.

In their determination to put an end to rustling, the Stock Growers had compiled a list of 70 men whom they were convinced were guilty. They formed a vigilante group, the Regulators, drawn from their supporters and ranch workers, but also brought in additional professional gunmen from Texas – or, in Canton's version, 'some brave and experienced officers'. The posse of about 50 men formed in Cheyenne and with their horses and a large supply of weapons and ammunition boarded a train for Casper. Telegraph wires were cut to disrupt communications, although two reporters accompanied the raid. In Casper they led their horses from the train (thus inspiring a moment of visual drama in several Westerns) and set off through the night, supported by supply wagons. It was April, and there was a light snow on the ground. Their destination was Buffalo, considered to be a rustlers' stronghold, but they diverted to the KC Ranch, when they heard a man identified as a ringleader of the rustlers, Nathan Champion, and his partner Nick Ray (or Rae, an Orkney name), were hiding out there. The Regulators arrived before daylight, and surrounded the log cabin in which the men were holed up. When dawn came, the firing started.

Ray attempted to run from the cabin, but was shot down. Champion rushed out in a hail of bullets and succeeded in dragging his partner back to safety, but Ray died soon after. The besiegers continued to pour bullets into the cabin. 'The only thing we could do,' wrote Canton, 'was to pour lead into the portholes [which the defendants had cut into the walls], but as fast as we drove him from one position, he would open up from another.' Eventually it was decided to fire the cabin, and the pine logs were soon ablaze. When Champion made a dash for safety he was instantly shot down, an episode reminiscent of events in the Lincoln County War. In the pocket of the dead man's shirt a notebook was found, in which Champion had recorded his final hours. 'I feel pretty lonesome just now,' he wrote. 'I wish there was someone here with me so we could watch all sides at once.' Frank Canton generously commented: 'If he had been fighting in a good cause, he would have been a hero.'

With Ray and Champion dead, the Regulators moved on

towards Buffalo, where the sheriff was William ('Red') Angus, a
Scot believed to be friendly to the homesteaders and therefore to
rustlers. But the Regulators never got there. They were met by a
motley and very angry crowd of at least a hundred volunteers. (Some
accounts say 300, and some no doubt were rustlers. According to
Jon E. Lewis in his book *The West* (1998), there were clergymen
among them.) They were armed with pitchforks, clubs and rifles,
and the invaders turned tail. In a barn at the TA Ranch, the
besiegers became the besieged, bullets splintering the barn walls.
For two days the Regulators fended off the angry volunteers, short
of ammunition and food and water as they had abandoned the wagons in their flight. (Canton's account makes no mention of flight,
and states that they had time to dig trenches and lay in supplies of
drinking water and beef.)

Eventually one of the besieged managed to slip through the lines
of the homesteader force and get word to Casper and then to
Cheyenne. From there, urgent messages went to Washington.
Meanwhile, Sheriff Angus rode for Fort McKinney to enlist the help
of troops stationed there. Early the next morning, just as a wagon
loaded with dynamite was rolling down towards the barn, 'the notes
of "Boots and Saddles" sounded in the clear dawn' as the cavalry led
by Colonel Van Horne and accompanied by Red Angus arrived. It
was, wrote historians Horan and Sann, 'strictly Hollywood'.

The 50 men were arrested and escorted to Fort Russell near
Cheyenne. 'Wolcott and his army had to surrender ingloriously,'
wrote John Clay. They spent the summer under guard – a costly
business – while arguments and manoeuvrings over their trial went on.
Johnson County struggled to bring a case against them: witnesses
mysteriously disappeared, and ultimately the county ran out of
money. In January 1893, Wolcott's army was free. Among them were
Joseph Elliot, William Irvine, William Guthrie, Charles Campbell,
Benjamin Morrison, W.B. Wallace, William Armstrong and Alexander
Hamilton: all Scottish names. Several of those who overtly or tacitly
colluded in their enterprise were also Scots.

John Clay states that it cost the cattle ranchers about $100,000, but, he added:

> ... money counts for little when placed beside nobility of character, of patient self-denial, of loyal friendship – the strong supporting the weak morally and financially. From this fiery furnace of trial and tribulation came pure gold, no tawdry counterfeit, but the real stuff, represented by splendid examples of courage, honesty, and everlasting belief in the justice of their cause.

He acknowledges that the killing of Nate Champion and Nick Ray was 'brutal', but it is quite clear that he considered the 'invasion' of Johnson County both justified and beneficial. Frank Canton added to the self-justification: 'It never has been any trouble since to convict a cattle thief in Johnson County. We made it safe for an honest man to live in that county and enjoy the fruits of his labor...' He maintained that when he had paid his share of the expenses, he had 'nothing left'.

In spite of the claims by Clay and Canton, evidence suggests that rustling continued to be a problem. The life and death of Tom Horn, linked with several Scottish American ranchers, provides a significant afterword. Horn, from Missouri, had tried his hand at all kinds of frontier jobs – stage driver, teamster, army scout, miner, railroad worker – before being hired by the Pinkerton Agency in Denver, where he worked with William Pinkerton and James McParland. In his memoir, in which he describes himself as 'government scout and interpreter', he says that in spite of the Agency being 'one of the greatest institutions of the kind in existence', working for it was 'too tame'. In 1892, he was taken on as a range detective by the Wyoming Stock Growers. Although he helped to recruit gunmen he was not directly involved in the Johnson County War. However, in 1894 he was hired by the Swan Land and Cattle Company (managed by Clay), ostensibly as a horse breaker but probably to track down rustlers.

After serving with the army in the Spanish-American War,

where he was with Theodore Roosevelt at San Juan Hill, Horn returned to Wyoming and again was employed as a range detective. The clash between small and big ranchers was still intense, and in the Iron Mountain country where Horn was operating there were, according to an account by the local schoolteacher, 'probably ... more rustlers to the square inch than any other place twice its size'. The rustlers were 'ignorant, shiftless and vicious'. When the young son of a homesteader was shot, Tom Horn was accused of the crime and convicted, although there were many who claimed that he could not have been guilty. He attempted to escape from jail with a fellow-prisoner called Jim McCloud, but was recaptured, and hanged on 20 November 1903.

Range wars have provided the theme for countless Westerns, but one in particular drew its inspiration from the Johnson County War: *Heaven's Gate*, directed by Michael Cimino (1980). Cimino's interpretation highlights the multi-ethnic nature of immigration to the West, depicting the homesteaders as coming largely from Eastern Europe and making a valiant attempt to resist the corporate power of the big ranchers. With one or two exceptions, the membership of the Stock Growers' Association is Anglo-Saxon (including the Scots). The classic 'big guys' versus 'little guys' Western is *Shane*, the original story by Jack Schaefer, the Western directed by George Stevens (1953) with a screenplay by A.B. Guthrie. The young boy who tells the story, son of the homesteader who is helped by Shane, the mysterious lone horseman, is called Robert MacPherson Starrett. The setting is Wyoming, 1889, when the opening skirmishes of the Johnson County War were already taking place.

In many Westerns, pressure on resources emerges as smaller-scale contests for land and property. This is the case in T.T. Flynn's *Riding High* (1961), in which a brutish ranch foreman – 'a massive, malevolent figure' – tries to bully his way to power. His name is Con McCloud. Other Scottish names appear in the story. Flynn is better known as author of *The Man from Laramie*, which was filmed by Anthony Mann in 1956. Its hero is Will Lockhart (a Scottish name) who is played by James Stewart. He is a very different figure from McCloud. As a loner seeking vengeance, operating outwith conventional society and outwith the law, he is, like Shane, a classic version of the Western hero. Clint Eastwood's Stranger (aka Jim Duncan) in *High Plains Drifter* is another take on the same theme.

In the second half of the 19th century, immigrants were pouring in from all over Europe, and Scots were finding themselves side by side with communities who may have shared something of their experience of the old country, but whose languages and traditions were alien. *Heaven's Gate* highlights the privileged position of native English speakers. Although we know there were Gaelic speakers in the West, they are not found in Westerns, although a memory of Gaelic is an important feature of the novels of the Canadian West by Margaret Laurence. She also explores the juxtaposition between immigrants of different origins, writing about relations between Scottish and Ukrainian communities in Manitoba.

Those who first helped themselves to open range in Montana and Wyoming, men such as Granville Stuart and the ranchers John Clay represented, considered they had a right to the land, as they were the pioneers who made it habitable and safe. Although not necessarily unsympathetic to the Native American population, they embodied the conviction that profit from the land's resources was deserved by those prepared to work and in some cases to risk their lives to exploit them. The profoundly different Native under-standing of relationship with the land had no place in this scheme of things. This was a quintessentially American belief which became stronger than ever in the second half of the 19th century. The immigrants who poured in after the Civil War put unprece-dented pressure on space and the land's productivity, and helped to trigger the final chapter in the suppression of the Native population as well as range wars. The climax of the Johnson County War came not much more than a year after Wounded Knee.

John Clay had left Scotland to make something of the

opportunities offered by the United States. He wasn't going to give up what he felt he had worked hard for, even if holding on meant denying opportunity to others. Clay, like his more famous country-man Andrew Carnegie, embodied the paradox at the heart of the land of opportunity. By the end of the 19th century it was clear that the vast country's resources were not limitless, and that the success of an individual or a business, whether cattle or steel, was inevitably built on the exclusion of others.

The after effects of the Johnson County War lasted well into the 20th century, and there is still debate about the roles of various individuals and the morality of their actions. Although men like Clay and Canton argued that Wyoming was a safer and more law-abiding place as a consequence of vigilante efforts, the 'invasion' divided communities and left a legacy of resentment and distrust. The local press was on the whole critical of the big ranchers, and championed the 'little guys' who had little influence, but the 'big guys' made sure their version was strongly presented. The tensions did not dissipate, and the settlers kept coming. When the Doig family made their way from Dundee to Montana soon after the Johnson County War, they must have heard tales of conflict and sudden death. But they had other, more urgent difficulties to contend with as they struggled to establish themselves on what was left of the frontier.

CHAPTER 10

Wilderness

The pretty valley stretched beyond,
The mountains towered above.

'California', Captain Jack Crawford

WHEN IN 1861 Henry Thoreau wrote 'we go westward as into the future, with a spirit of enterprise and adventure', thousands of emigrants had done exactly that, reaching as far west as it was possible to go without leaving the continent. Tens of thousands would follow. Thoreau himself never got further than Minnesota, but he argued that there was a natural westward pull, following the direction of the sun. In the American context, the frontier had moved from east to west, which seemed to confirm his thesis. For most of those who submitted to the pull, the West was indeed 'but another name for the wild', as Thoreau put it, and western migrants were prepared for wildness, and to an extent wanted it. Some of the Scots among them would have had some experience of wildness themselves, but many had not. Wilderness may have offered opportunity, but it also demanded the employment of particular skills, and not all were appropriately equipped.

Decades earlier, Scots had been involved in exploring and recording the North American wilderness. The best known Scottish explorers were mapping the far north – Alexander Mackenzie, Robert Campbell in the Yukon, John Rae in the Arctic – but others were making a significant contribution south of what became the Canadian border. David Douglas was born in Scone, Perthshire in 1799, son of a stone mason. He became gardener at Scone Palace, then assistant to Professor William Hooker at Glasgow Botanic Garden before being sent across the Atlantic by London's Royal

Horticultural Society. He made three collecting expeditions to North America. It was his second expedition, in 1825, which took him round Cape Horn to the mouth of the Columbia River, that yielded the richest results and led to the Douglas fir being introduced in Scotland from seeds he sent home. It was only one of 200 species that he brought to Britain from the Pacific Northwest and California. On one of his solo collecting trips in Oregon he was surprised by Indians who came upon him closely examining trees. They called him 'Man of Grass'.

Driven by enthusiasm and sustained by what seemed a natural and matter-of-fact spirit of endurance, Douglas tramped around ten thousand miles, often alone, in his efforts to collect and record American species. He did not question the need to take risks: 'Such objects as I am in quest of,' he wrote, 'are not obtained without a share of labour, anxiety of mind and sometimes risk of personal safety.' There were times when he found himself without food or shelter, exposed to foul weather. On one occasion he was descending the Fraser River when he encountered rapids which smashed his canoe. His notes and specimens were all lost. At the age of only 35 he died in a gruesome accident, gored by a bull in Hawaii.

Travelling with Douglas for a short time was Thomas Drummond, also from Perthshire. He had been assistant naturalist to Sir John Franklin's second Arctic expedition so was familiar with rugged country. He also botanised in Texas, and many of the specimens collected by him were sent to Glasgow's Botanic Garden. William Tolmie, a Glasgow doctor who emigrated to Oregon in 1833, was an associate of John McLoughlin at Fort Vancouver, and had extensive interests in horticulture and stock raising. As well as collecting plants with the help of John McLeod, the Scottish-born fur trader who had assisted the Whitmans on their journey through the Rockies, he was manager of the Puget Sound Agricultural Company. Its object was to cultivate crops to help feed Hudson's Bay Company employees. Tolmie also brought Scottish sheep to Oregon.

Writing in the early 1830s, Washington Irving, moved perhaps by the Orcadian blood in his veins, expressed a wish to travel west before the wilderness disappeared, as he believed it inevitably would. He wanted to 'see those fine countries of the "far west", while still in a state of pristine wilderness, and behold herds of buffaloes scouring their native prairies, before they are driven beyond the reach of the civilised tourist'. For him, as for many others, wild spaces represented a kind of freedom, an escape from a conventional existence weighed down by material things: 'Our superfluities are the chains that bind us, impeding every movement of our bodies and thwarting every impulse of our souls.' It was at this time that Charles Augustus Murray, second son of the 5th Earl of Dunmore, set off from Fort Leavenworth on the Missouri on an expedition to meet the Pawnee – 'genuine children of the wilderness' – and learn something of their way of life. He travelled in the Indian manner, rising before dawn and riding for hours without food. He was welcomed by a tribe of around 5,000 Pawnees, joined in their buffalo hunts, tasted raw buffalo liver, and experienced a Cheyenne attack. He relished his western adventures and took a real interest in his Pawnee companions, whom he described in some detail in his book *Travels in North America* (1854).

Murray enjoyed the wilderness, but missed his home comforts and was glad to return to Fort Leavenworth. He was intrigued by Native Americans, and both intrigued and impressed by the settlers who were transforming the frontier states. He found there a 'real republican equality', which he felt had been eroded further east:

> In the Far West, where society is in its infancy, where all are engaged in making money by bringing into cultivation waste lands, or raising minerals, – where men of leisure are unknown, and the arm of the law is feeble in protecting life and property, – where the tone of manners, conversation, and accomplishment, is necessarily much lower than in states and cities longer established, – here it is that true republican equality exists, and here only can it exist.

For Murray, the attraction of the frontier was precisely that it was rough and ready. He does not comment on the fact that the activities he describes were part of the process of destroying the wilderness and the people who inhabited it, and preparing the way for the community building Washington Irving describes.

The 1830s saw the arrival in the West of another second son of the Scottish aristocracy. In 1833 Perthshire-born William Drummond Stewart joined Robert Campbell and a party of fur traders making their way to the annual rendezvous, where trappers assembled to trade their year's work. It was the first of several trips. Stewart was a former soldier who had fought at Waterloo, and he knew how to make himself useful. The mule train loaded with trade goods assembled at Lexington, Missouri, and followed the River Platte to the rendezvous on Green River. Stewart was an enthusiastic participant in all aspects of frontier life, especially hunting, but, like Murray, he enjoyed his comforts. He travelled with ample supplies of good food, wine and brandy, which he generously shared with his companions. He was a keen player in the two or three weeks of unrestrained carousing, which characterised the rendezvous, the annual release for men who had spent most of the year without female companionship, and sometimes without companionship of any kind. William Gray, a Presbyterian cabinet maker, met Stewart in 1836 and described him with a distinct note of disapproval: 'His general conversation and appearance was that of a man with strong prejudices and equally strong appetites, which he had freely indulged, with only pecuniary restraint.'

Another description comes from Englishman George Frederick Ruxton, whose semi-fictionalised *Life in the Far West* was first published in *Blackwood's Edinburgh Magazine* in 1848. His mountain man narrator was rather more impressed:

> He was no trader, nor trapper, and flung his dollars right smart. Thar was old grit in him, too, and a hair of the black b'ar at that...he had the best powder as ever I flashed through life, and his gun was handsome, that's a fact.

Stewart came to know William Sublette, Jim Bridger and William Clark (an Ulster Scot), and readily absorbed the spirit of frontier pioneers. He met John McLoughlin at Fort Vancouver and the Whitmans at their mission on the Columbia. Like John McLeod, he was particularly taken by Narcissa: 'What would I not give to possess her love and be at home in Scotland?'

In 1837 he met the artist Alfred Jacob Miller, and commissioned him to accompany his next trip to the Rockies. The result was nearly three hundred sketches of the landscape and people they encountered, some of which became the basis of full-scale paintings. Many of them featured Stewart himself, wearing the distinctive buckskin of the mountain man and riding a white horse. Some of the pictures were brought back to Perthshire, and hung in Murthly Castle which Stewart inherited in 1838 on the death of his older brother. He also arranged to have sent to Scotland several species of plains and mountain birds, plants and mammals – antelope, buffalo, bears and mountain goats. Murthly became famous for its herd of buffalo and its American trees.

Stewart made his last American expedition in 1843, and was present at the final fur trading rendezvous in the Wind River Mountains. The trade had dwindled, and the era of the mountain men was giving way to settled communities – the process so effectively chronicled in A.B. Guthrie's *The Big Sky* and *The Way West*. It was still possible to experience the wilderness as a 'tourist', but many of the distinctive features of the wild – not least the buffalo – would vanish over the next few decades.

Stewart returned to Murthly Castle, taking up the role of Scottish laird and never going back to the American West to witness these changes. He wrote two novels based on his experiences in the West, *Altowan, or Incidents of Life and Adventures in the Rocky Mountains* (1846) and *Edward Warren* (1854). Murray also wrote a novel, *The Prairie-Bird* (1844). Interestingly, these, along with Fenimore Cooper's *The Prairie* (1827), might be described as the first precursors of what became the Western.

For the committed seeker after wilderness it was still possible, after the last rendezvous of 1843, to find it. One such seeker was Isabella Bird who, though born in Yorkshire, lived in Scotland when she was not on the move. She made her first trips to the USA and Canada in the 1850s, but in the autumn of 1873 was back in the US, on a train climbing into the Sierras. She alighted at Truckee and set off alone on horseback to explore the area around Lake Tahoe:

> All was bright with that brilliancy of sky and atmosphere, that blaze of sunshine and universal glitter, which I never saw until I came to California, combined with an elasticity in the air which removed all lassitude, and gives one spirit enough for anything.

She was a seasoned traveller, not afraid to journey alone and undeterred when her horse was frightened by a bear and threw her. Neither was she deterred by the wild humanity she encountered. Truckee at night was typical of a mining camp and train depot, 'fires blazing out of doors, bar-rooms and saloons crammed, lights glaring, gaming tables thronged, fiddle and banjo in frightful discord, and the air ringing with ribaldry and profanity'. She was confident of frontier respect for women: 'womanly dignity and manly respect for women are the salt of society in this Wild West', and although she acknowledged there were plenty of ruffians about, 'the ugliest among them all won't touch you'.

In most people's eyes, Mountain Jim, whom she encountered in Colorado, qualified as one of the worst. He had, Isabella Bird wrote, '"desperado" written all over him'. Broad, thickset and one-eyed he was an alarming figure:

> [with] an old pair of high boots, with a baggy pair of old trousers made of deer hide, held on by an old scarf tucked into them; a leather shirt, with three or four ragged unbuttoned waistcoats over it; an old smashed wideawake, from under which his tawny, neglected ringlets hung; and with his one eye, his one long spur, his knife in his belt, his revolver in his waistcoat pocket, his saddle

covered with an old beaver skin, from which the paws hung down; his camping blankets behind him, his rifle laid across the saddle in front of him, and his axe, canteen, and other gear hanging to the horn, he was as awful-looking a ruffian as one could see.

Mountain Jim had been an Indian scout. Notoriously violent when drunk, he was 'a gentleman' when sober, and 'very courteous'. His beautiful and delicate Arab mare presented a striking contrast to his disreputable appearance, which did not prevent Bird taking him on as her guide in her explorations of the Colorado mountains.

She stayed for some time in the remote Estes Park, in the Front Range of the Rockies and not at all park-like in the British sense. It was an unsurveyed no-man's-land, and Bird was entranced by it. It was, she wrote, 'mine by right of love, appropriation, and appreciation; by the seizure of its peerless sunrises and sunsets, its glorious afterglow, its blazing noons, its hurricanes sharp and furious, its wild auroras, its glories of mountain and forest, of canyon, lake, and river'. Its teeming wildlife included mountain lion, grizzly bear, coyote, lynx, mink, marten as well as less dramatic species, and birds from the crested blue-jay to the eagle. 'May their number never be less, in spite of the hunter who kills for food; and the sportsman who kills and marauds for pastime': a prayer worthy of every conservationist. She lived in a rough cabin by Mirror Lake, where the snow blew in through chinks between the logs, and explored on her pony Birdie. When she left Estes Park, she rode to Denver alone, and then south to Colorado Springs through a snow storm:

> I cannot describe my feelings on this ride, produced by the utter loneliness, the silence and dumbness of all things, the snow falling quietly without wind, the obliterated mountains, the darkness, the intense cold, and the unusual and appalling aspect of nature. All life was in a shroud, all work and travel suspended. There was not a foot-mark or a wheel mark.

Isabella Bird was 42 when she made this trip. Her account of her Rocky Mountain experiences was written first as letters to her sister in Scotland, then published in 1878 in the English weekly magazine *Leisure Hour*. The following year they appeared as a book, *A Lady's Life in the Rocky Mountains*. Although she responded to the grandeur of the landscapes she encountered with an almost romantic appreciation, her approach to her travels was practical as well as independent. She calmly accepted the realities of frontier life, describing without complaining, and confident of her ability to cope. She rode astride, having devised an outfit which allowed her to do this in comfort. Her 'American Lady's Mountain Dress', as she called it, consisted of 'a half-fitted jacket, a skirt reaching to the ankles, and full Turkish trousers gathered into frills which fall over the boots – a thoroughly serviceable and feminine costume for mountaineering and other rugged travelling in any part of the world.'

Six years before Isabella Bird embarked on her Rocky Mountain adventure, the young John Muir left his home in Wisconsin with a change of clothes and copies of Burns's poetry, the New Testament and *Paradise Lost* in his pack. He was heading southeast. But his long term aim was to go to California, not in pursuit of gold or riches, or at least not material riches, but to witness and feel for himself what his biographer Frederick Turner has described as 'the very newest part of this New World'. Muir was leaving behind the Wisconsin farm he had laboured on so hard as a boy under the eye of his tyrannical father. Daniel Muir's belief that hard graft and corporal punishment were a necessary part of rearing children had not destroyed his son's spirit. Unfazed by the 'heartbreaking chopping, grubbing, stump-digging, rail-splitting, fence-building, barn-building, house-building', John and his brother found the time and inclination to immerse themselves in a wild environment. Their schooldays at an end, they learnt from the natural world:

> Nature streaming into us, wooingly teaching her wonderful glowing lessons, so unlike the dismal grammar ashes and cinders so long thrashed into us. Here without knowing it we were still at school; every wild lesson a love lesson, not whipped but charmed into us. Oh, that glorious Wisconsin wilderness.

Wisconsin had become a territory in 1836, with a white population of 11,000. By 1850, the population was over 300,000; 10 years later that figure had more than doubled. But attitudes to land were profligate – there seemed so much of it. After eight years of relentless toil to clear the land and get established, the soil of the Muirs' Fountain Lake farm was exhausted and they moved on, though not very far, to start all over again.

Although Muir's relationship with his father was difficult, from an early age he practised the same severe self-discipline. Encouraged by neighbours, he read secretly and voraciously, getting up in the middle of the night to fit in time to read and to practise his discovered skills in mechanical invention, in particular clock-making. He left home to take some classes at the University of Wisconsin, and met people who recognised his abilities. Deeply disturbed by the slaughter of the Civil War, he abandoned his studies to escape the draft by crossing into Canada. There, working when he had to, he went on 'long, lonely excursions, botanising in glorious freedom around the Great Lakes'. At the heart of everything he did was his total immersion in the natural world. He wanted above all else to experience everything America's wilderness had to offer.

It was August 1867 when he left Wisconsin on the famous 1,000-mile walk that marked the beginning of a long adventure. He headed south and east, covering around 25 miles a day, and taking, as he wrote to a friend, the 'wildest, leafiest, and least trodden way'. He crossed the Cumberland Mountains into Pennsylvania, carried on south through Virginia and the Carolinas, where he encountered descendants of Scottish settlers living lives that seemed to be trapped in a previous century. He didn't have to go west to find wild mountain country and wild mountain people. His destination was Florida, where he took ship for Cuba.

From Cuba he returned north, this time to New York on the first stage of a journey that would take him to California, where he would spend most of the rest of his life and make his deepest mark. He went by sea to Panama, by train across the isthmus, then boat again to San Francisco. He took off at once for the mountains, on foot. He and an English companion headed south, then struck east to cross the Diablo Range and entered the San Joaquin Valley. At the top of the pass through the mountains Muir got his first sight of the snow-covered peaks of the Sierra Nevada. They walked on, into the Sierras and Yosemite. 'We are now in the mountains and they are in us,' he wrote, 'kindling enthusiasm, making every nerve quiver.'

They returned to San Joaquin. Although he claimed that the trip had cost him just $3, he needed to find employment. He tried various short-term jobs, then settled to work on a sheep ranch. 'I know that I could under ordinary circumstances accumulate wealth and obtain a fair position in society,' he wrote in a letter home, 'and have arrived at an age that requires that I should choose some definite course for life. But I am sure that the mind of no truant schoolboy is more free and disengaged from all the grave plans and purposes and pursuits of ordinary orthodox life than mine.' Like so many people of the frontier, Muir was escaping 'ordinary, orthodox life'; unlike most, he would make something quite extraordinary of his escape.

Over the next years Muir explored the mountains, usually alone, observing, collecting and recording. He travelled on horseback as far as the timberline, then on foot, taking with him minimal supplies – porridge, tea and bread – and the instruments he needed for his work: watch, pocket-lens, clinometer (for measuring slopes and elevation), aneroid barometer, thermometer, compass, pocket knife and spectacles. These expeditions were physically demanding, often dangerous, and lonely. But the loneliness was probably an essential part of the experience. Nothing got in the way of his intense and intimate response to the natural world – the mountains themselves and their formation, the trees and plants and flowers, the animals:

> As long as I live, I'll hear waterfalls and birds and winds sing. I'll interpret the rocks, learn the language of the flood, storm, and the avalanche. I'll acquaint myself with the glaciers and wild gardens, and get as near the heart of the world as I can.

He made Yosemite his own. In 1871 he entered the Hetch Hetchy Valley for the first time. He climbed Mt Ritter and Mt Whitney, the latter as part of an 1873 1,000-mile trip into the High Sierras. He was confident in his ability to handle whatever nature put in his way: 'In any sudden exigency a sound man brought face to face with danger will always do better than he anticipates.'

He began to publish accounts of his experiences and observations. From his first explorations, he was acutely aware not only of the detail of landscape and the life it nurtured, but of the impact of man. The gold rush had come and gone, leaving 'dead mining towns, with their tall chimney-stacks, standing forlorn amid broken walls and furnaces, and machinery half buried in the sand'. Increasing numbers of sheep were cropping and destroying the vegetation. Vast quantities of timber were being felled. Water courses were being altered. More and more he began to feel that the wilderness, which was integral to what defined America, had to be protected from the depredations of American striving for productivity.

In 1864, part of Yosemite had been designated a state park, but there was no adequate protection from human activity. The dominant American view was that public land and natural resources were there to be exploited, and that attempts to limit this were a restriction of freedom. Yellowstone had become a national park in 1872, and the Adirondacks in New York State designated 'forever wild' in 1885, but the notion of powerful safeguarding of the wilderness was yet to take hold. It took a determined campaign, spearheaded by Muir and Robert Underwood Johnson, editor of the *Century* magazine where Muir's articles were published, to achieve in 1890 the creation of Yosemite National Park. 'Unless reserved or protected the whole region will soon or late be devastated by lumbermen and sheepmen,' wrote Muir. The wilderness was vital as a source of refreshment and renewal. In the wilderness 'lies the hope of the world – the great fresh unblighted, unredeemed wilderness'. Two years later Muir and others founded the Sierra Club, with Muir as its first president, to 'enlist the support and co-operation of the people and the government in preserving the forests and other features of the Sierra Nevada Mountains'.

Muir had married Louie Strentzel in 1880, and embarked on a new career running the fruit farm at Martinez in the Alhambra Valley that had been started by her parents. He was an energetic and committed farmer, and put to good use his practical skills and experience. He was also a shrewd businessman. The farm did well, and Muir made money. But he could not give up the wilderness. He continued to make expeditions into the mountains, and made two trips to Alaska. He returned to Scotland in 1893, to Edinburgh first and then Dunbar, where he visited old acquaintances and wandered the town. He walked again in the nearby Lammermuirs, where he had first learnt to respond to the wild. 'I am a Scotchman and at home again,' he wrote in a letter to Louie in California. On the rocks and sand of the North Sea shore he listened to the sound of the waves: 'I seemed a boy again,' he wrote to his daughter Wanda, 'and all the long years in America were forgotten while I was filled with that glorious ocean psalm.'

Back in California, Muir was campaigning for the preservation of the forests, which were being increasingly plundered for profit. America had once been 'a garden...favoured above all other parks and gardens of the world'. Its forests were 'rich beyond thought, enough and to spare for every feeding, sheltering beast and bird, insect and son of Adam', but the 'steel axe of the white man' had initiated destruction on an unimaginable scale. 'Any fool can destroy trees,' Muir wrote:

> They cannot run away; and even if they could, they would still be destroyed, – chased and hunted down as long as fun or a dollar could be got out of their bark hides, branching horns, or magnificent bole backbones.

Muir argued that trees and mountains and all the life they contained were valuable for their own sake and for the refreshment and renewal they offered humanity. He clashed with those who believed that they were resources to be conserved and managed for economic purposes. He lost the battle over San Francisco's plans to dam Hetch Hetchy Valley to provide water for the city, antagonising many in the process. The stress of the campaign took its toll, but it did not diminish his passionate belief in the richness and goodness of the natural world. 'It is always sunrise somewhere,' he wrote. Although he was often dismayed by the power of vested interests and exasperated with the obtuseness of those who failed to understand that 'the wilderness is a necessity', his message did not falter. It was a social message, but articulated with a simplicity that was profoundly personal. 'I only went out for a walk,' he wrote, in explaining his life, 'and finally concluded to stay out till sundown, for going out, I found, was really going in.'

In 1872, John Muir met another Scot who made his name in California. William Keith born in 1838 in Oldmeldrum, near Aberdeen, was an exact contemporary of Muir's. He had arrived in New York as a boy, and in 1857 found work as a wood engraver for the publishers Harper and Brothers. Two years later he was in San Francisco, where he continued to work as a wood engraver and began, as a self-taught artist, to paint landscapes. He sought out Muir in his Yosemite cabin and the two became close friends. Keith accompanied Muir on camping trips in the High Sierras and painted what he saw. Muir admired his ability to record scenes of wilderness in precise detail, but Keith gradually moved to a more suggestive, evocative style although he never lost his commitment to an accurate rendering of the natural world. He painted resonant panoramic landscapes, which proved extremely popular. By the end of the century he was considered a leading San Francisco artist, and had an income of around $100,000 a year.

Another Scottish artist, of a rather different kind, had close Californian connections. Robert Louis Stevenson, who arrived in California in 1879 after his punishing experience crossing the continent by train, also had a strong affinity with mountains. He chose to spend his honeymoon on top of one, in an abandoned mining camp in circumstances which might well have appealed to Muir, who married in the same year. Crossing the Nebraska Plains, Stevenson 'grew homesick for the mountains' although when they entered the Rockies, he found the landscape 'dreary' and 'God-for-saken', 'long sterile canyons' treeless and scattered with boulders. But when Stevenson's train finally pulled out of the 'fiery hot and deadly weary' Nevada desert into the Sierras he experienced huge relief at being among pine trees and the sound of waterfalls: 'the air struck chill, but tasted good and vigorous'. The next morning the train emerged from a snow-shed to offer a glimpse 'of a huge pine-forested ravine upon my left, a foaming river, and a sky already coloured with the fires of dawn'.

If the scale and intensity of California's mountain landscape was beyond anything Stevenson had experienced in Scotland, there was still a familiarity about it: 'I had come home again – home from unsightly deserts, to the green and habitable corners of the earth.' Muir did not share Stevenson's antipathy towards deserts – to him, every natural environment and habitat were to be celebrated – but he would have recognised Stevenson's engagement with the extremes of nature, both in Scotland and the United States. Stevenson knew Muir's North Sea coast well, and had also walked the Border hills. He was never robust enough in health to acquire Muir's wilderness skills, but he knew what it was like to be thrown on his own devices in wild country. (In a Scottish context, he captures this memorably in his novel *Kidnapped*, of 1886.) There is no evidence that the two men ever met.

While John Muir was devoting his efforts to protecting the wilder-ness, John McLaren, who grew up on a farm at Bannockburn near Stirling, was transforming a stretch of San Francisco scrub and sand dunes into the Golden Gate Park. It involved planting a million trees. He had been employed at Edinburgh's Royal Botanic Garden, then emigrated to California where he pursued a career as landscape gardener. In 1887 he was appointed superintendent of San Francisco's parks. He was just one of many Scottish gardeners who made a lasting mark on America.

In many ways, John Muir, whose Scottish identity profoundly shaped his character and his purpose in life, is an archetypal if unexpected Western hero. He was tough and self-sufficient. He relished the wilderness and acquired the skills to survive in it. All his senses were attuned to the sights and sounds of the natural world, and he knew how to interpret what he saw and heard. He could walk and ride for days with minimal nourishment and without fear. He didn't ride the range or shoot his way out of trouble, pan for gold in mountain rivers or play poker in seedy saloons, but he had been a toiling homesteader and he had a love of the land which permeates so much of Western literature, from dime novels to his own writing. And like the first Scots in the American West, he had forged new trails. Although in Britain it is only relatively recently that his crucial role in the American conservation movement has been recognised, in the US his achievement and legacy have been acknowledged for more than a century. His identity as a heroic frontiersman steeped in the pioneer experience has no doubt contributed to the American readiness to embrace him.

Like the mythic Western heroes, Muir's theme song could have been 'don't fence me in'. From colonial times, America seemed to offer the challenge of a limitless, unfenced land at a time when Europe was becoming increasingly enclosed and confined. The effect was often intoxicating, reflected in great American writers – Thoreau, Emerson, Whitman – as well as in the emigrant guides that were published in Scotland and spurred Scots to abandon the old country for the promise of a new. Western heroes passed into legend so rapidly because that last phase of the frontier lasted only a few short decades. It seemed that the environment of the self-sufficient loner was disappearing.

That self-sufficient loner was often of Scottish origin, in fact and in fiction. The distinctive Westerns of Anthony Mann feature heroes with Scottish names: Lin McAdam in *Winchester '73* (1950), Glyn McLyntock in *Bend of the River* (1952), Home Kemp in *The Naked Spur* (1953), Will Lockhart in *The Man from Laramie* (1955).

All of these characters are solitary, driven men, and of course they are all played by James Stewart. In military Westerns, Scottish names often appear: Major Amos Dundee in Peckinpah's *Major Dundee* (1964), and Lieutenant John Dunbar in *Dances with Wolves* (1990). A Scottish identity is reflected in villains as well as heroes, and in the names of ordinary folk who were at the heart of frontier experience.

Was the Scottish character particularly suited to frontier life? Indeed, can the Scottish character be usefully defined? Looking back at some of those who feature in these pages, I think the answer to both these questions is 'yes'. If thousands left Scotland out of desperation, feeling that they had no choice but to seek survival in another land, a large number of even the most disheartened were prepared for a demanding existence. Some clearly had an affinity with frontier wilderness. Many were pragmatic and stoical as travellers and settlers. A substantial number made good lives for themselves and their families on the western frontier. A few were impressively successful, and a few more achieved fame through dubious or unlawful activities.

Many pioneer Scots were sustained by religious conviction, and by a belief that their efforts would be rewarded, spiritually if not materially. It helped to combat loneliness as well as hardship. Scots generally believed in the value of education and of practical skills. Self-reliance is often a feature of Scottish character, as is a strong sense of kinship and community. The help that John Muir's family received from neighbouring emigrant Scots was typical. Scottish experience in many areas – engineering, agricultural technology, banking and commerce, subsistence farming, military action – was, as much by happenstance as anything else, of specific value to the developing US. It was often a mutually beneficial relationship.

In his novel *English Creek* (1984), Ivan Doig describes a Montana community of emigrant Scots, Germans, Norwegians and Missourians. At the centre of his story is the McCaskill family, who settled in an area known as Scotch Heaven. The original emigrant McCaskill was a stone mason from Arbroath who had worked for the famous Stevenson family of engineers, R.L. Stevenson's family. He came to Montana in the 1880s, along with Duffs, Barclays, Frews, Findlaters and Erskines – all from Scotland. The novel spans three generations. The young hero Jick comments on his father, the firstborn in a new country:

> Those firstborn always, always will live in a straddle between the ancestral path of life and the route of the new land. In my father's case the old country of the McCaskills, Scotland, was as distant and blank as the North Pole, and the fresh one, America, still was making itself. Especially a rough-edged part of America such as the Montana he was born into and grew up in.

The rough edges of frontier America accommodated a great variety of identities and nationalities, which in their turn contributed to the frontier character. The Scots that Doig describes – and he is drawing directly on the experience of his own family – hang onto aspects of their own identity, however distant the homeland. The Scottish accent survives, as do an oral memory of the old country and the experience of re-settlement. On the Fourth of July the community gets together for a celebratory rodeo, and dance Scotch reels on a floor scattered with oatmeal 'for better gliding'. There are constant references to the Scottish origins of the main characters.

Doig wrote several novels about this part of Montana, as well as his memoir *This House of Sky*, and in all these books his Scottish Americans appear as a natural part of the landscape and the rhythms of the pioneering inheritance. They are identifiably Scottish, yet deeply embedded in life in the American West, on the edge of a wilderness which sometimes defeats them. These are 20th-century ranchers and rangers, engaged in what is still an elemental struggle with environment and climate. That struggle was part of the Scottish as well as the pioneer inheritance.

Chronology

1803	Louisiana Purchase doubles size of USA
1804	Lewis and Clark expedition sets off from St Louis
1811	Astoria fur-trading post set up at mouth of Columbia River
1812	Robert Stuart crosses Rockies west to east through South Pass
1812–15	War between Britain and US
1821	Hudson's Bay Company and North West Company merge; Mexico gains independence from Spain
1823	David Douglas's first collecting trip to US; beginnings of Texas Rangers
1825	Fort Vancouver set up on Columbia River; first fur trappers' rendezvous on Green River
1827	Jedediah Smith crosses Sierras
1828	Fort Union set up on the Missouri; Andrew Jackson elected president
1832	Sam Houston goes to Texas
1833	William Drummond Stewart attends Green River rendezvous
1834	Fort Hall set up on Snake River; Fort Boise set up on confluence of Snake and Boise Rivers; pioneers make overland journey to Oregon
1835	Colt revolver patented
1836	Texas declares independence; the Alamo, San Antonio, falls to Mexican forces
1838	Cherokees and other tribes forced west from Georgia on the 'Trail of Tears'

1842	Oregon City founded by John McLoughlin on Willamette River; Elijah White leads wagon train to Oregon; Allan Pinkerton leaves Glasgow for Chicago
1843	Last fur trappers' rendezvous
1844	Invention of telegraph by Samuel Morse
1845	Texas joins US; US invades Mexico
1846	British give up claim to Oregon and Washington Territories; John Frémont secures California for US; Donner party sets off for California; Iowa and Utah join Union
1847	Mormons enter Salt Lake Valley
1848	Treaty of Guadalupe Hidalgo gives New Mexico and California to the US; discovery of gold in California; Fort Kearney set up on River Platte
1849	Muir family leaves Dunbar for Wisconsin; Wisconsin joins Union
1850	California joins Union
1857	John Stewart Kennedy begins financial career in US
1858	Overland stage route established; Minnesota joins Union
1859	Pike's Peak gold rush; Oregon joins Union
1860	Outbreak of American Civil War; Pony Express begins
1861	Kansas joins Union
1862	Homestead Act; Central Pacific and Union Pacific Railroads authorised by Congress
1863	President Lincoln gives Gettysburg Address
1864	Kit Carson escorts Navaho to reservation at Bosque Redondo; Nevada joins Union
1865	President Lincoln assassinated; General Lee surrenders at Appomattox courthouse

1867	Kansas Pacific Railroad reaches Abilene, Kansas; Chisholm Trail opened from Texas to Abilene; Nebraska joins Union
1868	Massacre of Cheyenne on Washita River by General Custer's 7th Cavalry
1869	Transcontinental railroad completed
1870	Scottish American Investment Trust set up
1871	John Muir explores Hetch Hetchy Valley
1873	Beginning of major Scottish investment in American West; Isabella Bird travels in the Rockies
1876	General George Armstrong Custer's troops defeated by Sioux at the Battle of the Little Bighorn; Wild Bill Hickok shot by Jack McCall; Colorado joins Union
1877	Surrender of Chief Joseph and Nez Perce; death of Crazy Horse; *The Scotsman* newspaper investigates American cattle industry
1878	Breakout of Cheyenne from reservation in Indian Territory; Lincoln County War
1879	Robert Louis Stevenson makes his emigrant journey to California; John Clay settles in Wyoming; Robert Cunninghame Graham starts ranching in Texas; Granville Stuart starts ranching in Montana
1881	Surrender of Sitting Bull; Scottish Pacific Coast Mining Company set up; Billy the Kid shot by Pat Garrett; gunfight at OK Corral
1882	Matador Land and Cattle Company set up; Arizona Copper Company set up; Jesse James shot by Bob Ford
1886	Apache chief Geronimo surrenders to General Crook
1886–7	Severe winter devastates cattle ranches in Montana and Wyoming

1889   Indian Territory opened for settlement, becomes Oklahoma; North and South Dakota join Union

1890   US Census announces that frontier is closed; death of Sitting Bull and massacre at Wounded Knee Creek; John Muir founds Yosemite National Park; Murdo Mackenzie takes over as manager of Matador Ranch; Idaho and Wyoming join Union

1891   Cripple Creek gold rush

1892   Johnson County War

1893   Great Northern Railroad to Seattle completed

1896   Glasgow and Western Exploration Company set up; Jumper Gold Syndicate founded by Glaswegians

1907   Oklahoma joins Union

Bibliography

Aspinwall, Bernard: *Portable Utopia: Glasgow and the United States*, Aberdeen, 1984

Atherton, Lewis: *The Cattle Kings*, Bloomington, 1962

Beebe, Lucius and Charles Clegg: *The Age of Steam*, New York, 1994

Bird, Isabella: *A Lady's Life in the Rocky Mountains*, London, 1982

Black, George F.: *Scotland's Mark on America*, New York, 1921

Bronson, Edgar: *Reminiscences of a Ranchman*, Lincoln, 1962

Brown, Dee: *The American West*, London, 2004
Bury My Heart at Wounded Knee, London, 1971

Bourke, John G.: *On the Border with Crook*, London, 1982

Calder, Jenni: *Scots in the USA*. Edinburgh, 2005
There Must be a Lone Ranger: The Myth and Reality of the American West, London, 1974

Campbell, Randolph B.: *Gone to Texas*, Oxford, 2003

Canton, Frank: *Frontier Trails: The Autobiography of Frank M. Canton*, ed. Edward Everett Dale, Norman, 1966

Clay, John: *My Life on the Range*, Norman, 1962

Clee, Paul: *Photography and the Making of the American West*, North Haven, 2003

Cohen, Michael: *The Pathless Way: John Muir and American Wilderness*, Madison, 1984

Cunningham, Tom: *The Diamond's Ace: Scotland and the Native Americans*, Edinburgh, 2001

Dakin, Susan Bryant: *A Scotch Paisano in Los Angeles*, 1978

DeVoto, Bernard: *Across the Wide Missouri*, New York, 1998

Doig, Ivan: *Bucking the Sun*, New York, 1996
English Creek, London, 1985
This House of Sky: Landscapes of the Western Mind, San Diego, 1992

Fast, Howard: *The Last Frontier*, London, 1966

Ferguson, Fergus: *From Glasgow to Missouri*, Glasgow, 1878

Gard, Wayne: *Frontier Justice*, Norman, 1949

Gibson, Rob: *Plaids and Bandanas: from Highland Drover to Wild West Cowboy*, Edinburgh, 2003

Graham, Hugh Davis and Ted Robert Gurr: *Violence in America: Historical and Comparative Perspectives*, New York, 1969

Graham, R.B. Cunninghame: *The North American Sketches*, ed. John Walker, Edinburgh, 1986

Guthrie, A.B. Jr: *The Big Sky*, Chicago, 1980

  The Blue Hen's Chick, Lincoln, 1993

  The Way West, New York, 1976

  These Thousand Hills, New York, 1971

Haycox, Ernest: *Free Grass*, New York, 1958

  Canyon Passage, London, 1967

Hewitson, Jim: *Tam Blake & Co: The Story of the Scots in America*, Edinburgh, 1993

Hill, James J.: *Highways of Progress*, London, 1910

Horan, James D.: *The Pinkertons: The Detective Dynasty that Made History*, New York, 1967

Horan, James D. and Paul Sann: *Pictorial History of the Wild West*, London, 1961

Horn, Tom: *Life of Tom Horn, Government Scout and Interpreter, Written by Himself*, Norman, 1964

Hunter, James: *A Dance Called America*, Edinburgh, 1994

  Glencoe and the Indians, Edinburgh, 1996

Irving, Washington: *Astoria: Adventure in the Pacific Northwest*, London, 1987

  A Tour on the Prairies, ed. John Frances McDermott, Norman, 1985

Lavender, David: *The Penguin Book of the American West*, Harmondsworth, 1969

  Westward Vision: The Story of the Oregon Trail, London, 1963

Leakey, John: *The West that Was, from Texas to Montana*, as told to Nellie Snyder Yost, Lincoln, 1958

Lewis, Jon E.: *The West: The Making of the American West*, Bristol, 1998

McCartney, Laton: Across *the Great Divide: Robert Stuart and the Discovery of the Oregon Trail*, Stroud, 2003

McGrath, Roger: *Gunfighters, Highwaymen and Vigilantes*, Berkeley, 1982

MacInnes, Allan, Marjory-Ann D. Harper and Linda G. Fryer: *Scotland and the Americas, c.1650–c.1939*, Edinburgh, 2002

Mackay, Alexander: *The Western World and Travels in the US 1846 and 1847*, 1849

Mackay, Charles: *Life and Liberty in America*, London 1859

McLynn, Frank: *Wagons West*, London, 2002

MacRae, David: *America Revisited*, Glasgow, 1908

Martin, Albro: *James J. Hill and the Opening of the Northwest*, New York, 1976

Miller, Sally: *John Muir: Life and Work*, Albuquerque, 1993

Muir, John: *The Story of My Boyhood and Youth*, ed. Frank Tindall, Edinburgh, 1987

Murray, Charles Augustus: *Travels in North America*, London, 1945

O'Connor, Richard: *Wild Bill Hickok*, London, 1959

Oliphant, Laurence: *Minnesota and the Far West*, Edinburgh, 1855

O'Neal, Bill: *The Pimlico Encyclopedia of Western Gunfighters*, London, 1998

Osgood, Ernest Staples: *The Day of the Cattleman*, Chicago, 1939

Preston, Richard Arthur: *For Friends at Home: A Scottish Emigrant's Letters from Canada, California and the Cariboo 1844–1864*, Montreal, 1974

Raban, Jonathan: *Bad Land: An American Romance*, London, 1996

Ross, Alexander: *Adventures of the First Settlers on the Oregon or Columbia River*, London, 1849

Ross, Peter: *The Scot in America*, New York, 1896

Ruxton, George Frederick: *Life in the Far West*, ed. LeRoy R. Haten, Norman, 1964

Sandoz, Mari: *Cheyenne Autumn*, London, 1953

Schaefer, Jack: *Shane*, London, 1963

Stegner, Wallace: *The Gathering of Zion: The Story of the Mormon Trail*, London, 1966

Stevenson, R.L.: *From the Clyde to California: Robert Louis Stevenson's Emigrant Journey*, ed. Andrew Noble, Aberdeen, 1985

Stewart, George R.: *Ordeal by Hunger: The Story of the Donner Party*, London, 1962 [1936]

Stuart, Granville: *Forty Years on the Frontier, as seen in the Journals and Reminiscences of Granville Stuart, Gold-miner, Trader, Merchant, Rancher and Politician*, ed. Paul C. Phillips, Cleveland, 1925

Szasz, Ferenc: *Scots in the North American West 1790–1917*, Norman, 2000

Unruh, John D.: *The Plains Across: Emigrants, Wagon Trains and the American West*, London, 1992

Van Every, Dale: *The Final Challenge: The American Frontier 1804–1845*, New York, 1964

Van Vugt, William: *Britain to America: Mid-nineteenth Century Immigrants to the United States*, Chicago, 1999

Ward, Jean M. and Maveety, Elaine A. (eds.): *Pacific Northwest Women 1815–1925*, Corvallis, 1995

Wellman, Paul I.: *Death on the Prairie*, New York, 1954

A Note on Names

ALTHOUGH MANY OF THE PEOPLE who feature in this book are of known Scottish origins, there are some for whom only the names are a guide as to their identity. The following are all the surnames mentioned which I know to be or have assumed to be Scottish. In addition, there are without doubt people from Scotland who have been overlooked in my account because their names are Irish; and many Scottish names vanished when women married. It should also be noted that the spelling of some Scottish names was Americanised: for example McCloud.

A

Abercrombie
Adamson
Aikman
Alexander
Allan
Allison
Anderson
Angus
Armstrong

B

Bain
Baird
Barclay
Baxter
Bennett
Blackie
Blair
Borthwick
Bothwell
Bowie
Brodie
Brown
Buchanan
Burnett
Burns

C

Calderwood
Caldwell
Calhoun
Cameron
Campbell
Carfrae
Cargill
Carnegie
Carson
Chambers
Chisholm
Chisum
Christie
Clark
Clay
Coats
Coburn
Colquhoun
Craib
Craig
Crain
Crawford
Crockett
Crook
Crooks
Cunningham
Custer

D

Doig
Dollar
Donahoe
Douglas
Drummond
Duff
Dunbar
Duncan
Dundee

E

Elgin
Elliot
Erskine

F

Fergus
Ferguson
Findlater
Findlay
Finlay
Finlayson
Fleming
Forbes
Ford
Forsyth
Fraser
Frew

G

Gibson
Gifford
Gilchrist
Gillespie
Gordon
Gowan
Graham
Grant
Gray
Gunn
Guthrie

H

Hamilton
Hanna
Hay
Henderson
Henry
Hill
Hogg
Horsburgh
Houston
Howison

I

Irvine
Irving

J
Jackson
James

K
Keith
Kemp
Kennedy

L
Laidlaw
Lamont
Lang
Lawrie
Lawson
Lindsay
Lockhart
Logan
Low

M
McAdam
McAllen
McArthur
McBain
McCall
McCaskill
McCaulley
McClellan
McClure
McCluskie
McConnell
McCulloch
McCutcheon
MacDonald
McDougall
McDowell
M'Ekron
McFadden
McFarlane
MacFie

McGee
McGinley
MacGregor
McInnis
McIntosh
McIver
Mack
Mackay
Mackenzie
McKinley
McLaglen
McLane
McLaren
McLaughlin
McLean
McLeod
Macloud
McLoughlin
Maclure
McLyntock
McMillan
McNab
McNeil
MacPherson
McRae
Macray
McSween
McTaggart
MacTavish
Marjoribanks
Maxwell
Meek
Melrose
Menzies
Minto
Mitchell
Moffat
Morrison
Morton
Muir
Murray

N
Nelson
Nimmo
Nisbett
Nixon

O
Oliphant
Oliver

P
Patterson
Philip
Phillips
Pinkerton

R
Rae
Ramsay
Rankin
Regan
Reid
Robertson
Ross

S
Scott
Simpson
Sinclair
Smith
Stephen
Stevenson
Stewart
Stuart
Sutherland

T
Tait
Taylor
Thomson
Tolmie

U
Urquhart

W
Wallace
Watson

Y
Younger

Index